S0-BYE-224

Rethinking People Management

Rethinking People Management

A New Look at the Human Resources Function

James G. Stockard

amacom A Division of
American Management Associations

Library of Congress Cataloging in Publication Data

Stockard, James G
Rethinking people management.

Includes index.
1. Personnel management. I. Title.
HF5549.S863 658.3 79-54851
ISBN 0-8144-5576-X

First Printing

To the brightest possible future for women and girls everywhere, and especially to those in my immediate family circle—

Nadene, Agnes, Ruth, Janet, Wilma, Susan, Kristin, Elizabeth, and Lillie

Preface

THIS BOOK is about the nation's personnel offices, the people who manage them, and the people who expect service from them. As a practitioner of the art of personnel administration since 1938, I see in it some serious imperfections and some notable advances. On balance, it appears to me to be a line of work in deep trouble with its constituencies.

Part I explores the nature of our personnel departments' troubles. The first chapter sets forth how I believe we personnel specialists view ourselves and where I believe we stand with our constituencies—top management, operating officials and supervisors, rank-and-file employees, and people looking for work.

The second chapter identifies what I have found to be the roots of our problems in personnel administration. Top management is assigned its due share of the responsibility for personnel office malpractice. Other root causes include deficiencies in personnel office leadership, program planning deficiencies, communication gaps, stunted growth of the profession and weaknesses in some of us practitioners, and weak internal management of personnel activities.

Chapter 3 presents a scenario of what I see happening to personnel administration unless the friends of this management specialty reform it. It is not a pretty picture. Unfortunately, entire organizations and industries suffer when their personnel offices malfunction. Both the private and public sectors are affected, in my judgment; neither has a clear superiority over the other in the manner in which human resources are acquired, developed, and utilized.

A comprehensive blueprint for reform is detailed in Part II. It is presented as a three-stage process: revamping the personnel department (Chapter 4); improving the scope and level of service (Chapter 5); and providing for the continuing growth and development of the personnel staff (Chapter 6). Mainline personnel functions and neglected functions are identified. A major thrust of the message pertains to the selection of the personnel director and the senior personnel staff. Specific suggestions are made for improving the personnel system's presence and responsiveness within the production and service setting. Chapter 7, which concludes Part II, is a 16-step procedure for getting the reform program started. It includes a provision for having some milestones put in place at the outset for measuring progress.

Part III is addressed primarily to the users of personnel offices. It makes specific suggestions to top management, line and staff officials, rank-and-file employees, and job applicants on how to make the personnel office best serve their needs.

This book is constructively critical of personnel administration. It has many ideas which more conventional personnel specialists will probably find shocking and unacceptable. For example, it advocates that as we attempt to reform personnel administration, those of us in senior positions call for a vote of confidence and, if necessary, abdicate in favor of a team of experienced production and service people who would serve a "tour of duty" at the pleasure of top management. Also, instead of having personnel administration function from a cloistered enclave, I would fragment it by placing some personnel desks in the traffic mainstreams of the organization and by deploying mobile personnel teams. I would make the personnel office into a staff of "preventive maintenance (people) technicians" to serve human resources needs in a manner comparable to that in which "preventive maintenance (machinery) technicians" serve machinery in industrial operations.

In conclusion, I would leave the thought with readers that as goes the "health" of the nation's personnel offices, so goes, perhaps, the health of the nation's business, industry, and government at all levels. It is urgent, therefore, that personnel administration not be treated as a hopeless cripple. It is time for rehabilitation and some enlightened redirection. This book can be useful to anyone in a position to reform or effectively use the services of a personnel system.

James G. Stockard

Contents

Part I

A Profession in Trouble

Chapter 1

Where We Stand

THIS CHAPTER looks at personnel administration with a constructively critical eye. It weighs what I regard as some pluses and minuses and strikes a balance on where I think we stand. You may disagree with some of my pro and con entries and still agree with the end conclusion, or you may disagree with the whole analysis. The purpose of the chapter is to stretch your thinking and to have you examine the need for some reforms which I believe you will want to support at least on a trial basis.

WHERE DO WE STAND WITH TOP MANAGEMENT?

The Washington Post, in a July 31, 1978, editorial, observed that productivity (average output per hour of labor) in the United States has undergone very disquieting changes. In the 1967–77 decade productivity in U.S. manufacturing did very poorly in international competition among a group of major industrial powers. A U.S. Department of Labor study showed the following increases for that decade: Japan, 107 percent; West Germany, 70 percent; Italy, 62 percent; Canada, 43 percent; Great Britain, 27 percent; and the United States, 27 percent. Since 1977, furthermore, productivity in the American economy has shown almost no increase.

The International Herald Tribune reported on August 15, 1978, that the United States is becoming less competitive in high-technology markets. No 35 mm cameras or color television sets are now manufactured in the United States, although we once dominated those markets. According to the article, we maintain a lead in only three high-technology areas: computers, the aerospace industry, and heavy electronics. Japan is spending huge sums to close the gap in the computer industry. The smaller, more innovative companies are generally the ones making the technological breakthroughs that still occur in American industry.

The economywide leveling of productivity and the decline of innovativeness in larger companies are factors for which personnel departments have to accept their due share of responsibility.

Top management hears from the personnel department that personnel is responsible for managing manpower planning and the acquisition, development, and utilization of human resources; that it endeavors to recruit, select, and place individuals of high potential in appropriate positions; and that it oversees the development of employees until they are capable of utilizing their talents and abilities in the most effective manner possible. If all this is true, then top management must be casting an eye in our direction as they read news items like those summarized above.

Obviously, there are other factors contributing to the bottom line on productivity and innovativeness. For example, when the budget for research and development in a company is greatly reduced, new product designs and production methods will surely be affected.

To get at a fair answer to the issue of how top management views the performance of your own personnel department, I am posing below a series of specific questions. I believe these are fair questions that any chief executive could, and should, ask periodically of his personnel staff.

Program. Have we developed a comprehensive, integrated program of personnel administration, and is it fully operational on the scale intended?

This is a key question. If the answer is affirmative, no other questions need be asked; however, in my judgment few, if any, personnel departments we know can truly say yes to the question. Therefore, consider some sharper questions such as the following.

Style. Are we coming to grips with the substantive (program) responsibilities of the personnel department, or is the major share of our time still dissipated over individual cases—new hires, transfers, promotions, job reclassifications, and dismissals?

It is easy to slide into the habit pattern of fighting the case backlog and giving one's full attention to the actions under pressure. This can devastate work on positive personnel programs. For example, if the employment office has no time left to plan, organize, and run positive recruitment campaigns to stimulate sources of supply in certain labor categories, it is hard put to fill vacancies except with walk-ins or through newspaper ads or calls to employment agencies. These sources may be all right on some occasions but should hardly be expected to be the best sources of qualified talent.

It should also be observed in this connection that the best

talent available may already be at work in some capacity in the organization itself. It takes a program-oriented personnel department to establish workable promotion-from-within programs to identify such talent and to systematically see that it gets to the attention of selecting officials.

Dynamism. Have we maintained a flexible, dynamic organizational format through which to administer the personnel department services, or has the organization tended to be a static, conventional pattern from year to year?

In my experience, the personnel department is the last department to have organizational realignments, regardless of how drastically the overall organization and program change. It presides over reorganizations, reductions in force, rapid expansions, and decentralizations, but it continues to do business at the same old stand. The pattern was set decades ago. Branches generally go by such names as employment, classification and pay administration, training, employee relations, and personnel operations (records, files, personnel actions and reports). There are minor variations from place to place in these branch names, with the greatest difference being in employee relations, which in many companies is called industrial relations.

As personnel specialists, we constantly advocate that more attention be given to job analysis as a solid basis for informed recruitment, selection, placement, position classification, training, and other personnel functions. Several landmark research projects in behavioral science have focused on the problems of productivity as related to motivation and morale.

Organizations frantically search for new leadership, for persons who are creative and innovative, and for managers who can cope with labor–management relations issues. Have you ever heard of a major personnel unit with job analysis, motivation, morale, leadership, creativity, or innovation in its title? In other words, do our organizational designations in the personnel department truly reflect our professional interest in, and commitment to, solving these fundamental problems?

Directions. What are our goals and objectives as personnel managers and specialists? Do we actually have some, or is it a case of drifting from day to day, waiting for the messenger to bring another basket of personnel action requests and for the telephone to start ringing incessantly? If we have goals and objectives, were they determined in close collaboration with our colleagues in operating departments, or did we think them up as narrative justification for the budget we had to defend some months ago? Has each goal been plotted with the critical path, milestones, staffing input, and funding, using some technique such as PERT?

I once knew a personnel man who often drifted about the building, always with a folder under his arm. He would tell you privately that the folder held nothing in the way of official business; it was merely to disguise the purpose of his travels about the building, which was to keep up his contacts. I believe many of us would be in the same category as this fellow if our goals and objectives were ever scrutinized.

Leadership. How well have our organizations done in picking the personnel director, and how well has he or she done in picking the heads of branches and other senior staff in the personnel department? Would the choices on the whole stand the test of "best qualified person available"?

Of the seven personnel directors I have seen in action at close range, only one was first rate. One was an alcoholic. One saw his role through the eyes of a case-oriented attorney, law being his real interest and the field to which he retired. Another was getting his kicks out of being a professor of personnel administration at a night school, and he did poorly on the job. One was strictly a patronage and nepotism dispenser. Another engaged in high strategy on a political plane with top management and left personnel administration to an inherited staff which was marginal in spots. One director was doing the job to serve out a tour of duty without any commitment to personnel administration. One out of the seven persons I have in mind, the only female of the group, consistently did the personnel director job with highest distinction.

My honest appraisal of the senior staffs of these personnel officials is that many of them were misplaced and their performance was as spotty as their bosses'. Among scores of other personnel directors I have known less well, one of seven is a safe bet on the numbers who have been a good fit for the job and whose performance has been outstanding.

Personnel administration at home. To what extent have personnel departments practiced modern concepts of personnel administration within their own departments? Have we recruited, selected, placed, developed, utilized, promoted, and separated employees from the staff in accordance with the principles we advocate to operating officials? Unfortunately, I am afraid our answer has to be hedged, and an impartial investigator would find that we haven't.

Personnel offices have frequently been used as "parking lots" for individuals who couldn't make it in another spot but who were in the category of untouchables for one reason or another. This has not helped morale of more deserving staff members, and it has not contributed to the image of the personnel department or to the level of service rendered by it.

Management practices. Have we installed and practiced good management methods in the personnel department? Have such processes as planning, organizing, staffing, budgeting, delegation, control, coordination, and reporting been systematically applied? Are decision making and problem solving done as logically and with the skill and timing used by production, marketing, and financial managers? Is there accountability for results according to predetermined objectives? Are we doing enough research? Innovating? Model building? Pretesting? Follow-through? Quality control?

Again, my own feeling is that we rate a fairly low score on these questions. Aside from the internal state of affairs in the personnel department, we need to look at our impact on the quantity, quality, and manner of performance of the parent organization's total labor force. The next few questions do that.

Impact on organization and management. What is the net impact on the effort we are making to improve organization and management? Does the voice of our personnel director or his staff count when adjustments in organization and management methods and controls are instituted?

Quest for leadership. Are we participating to any appreciable degree in the selection and development of new leadership for policy-making positions and in the selection, placement, and development of middle managers?

Labor–management involvement. Do we have a prominent role in labor–management affairs, or is it definitely a "water boy" role? Do we help formulate management's final offer to labor, or do we merely arrange for the printing and distribution of the agreement after agreements are reached by both sides?

Contributions to productivity. Can we honestly take any credit for improvements that have been made in productivity, morale, turnover, safety, or incentives?

Fiscal policy. Are we influencing the organization's overall budget planning and execution? Can we show any improvement in the profit or service position of the organization as a direct result of personnel administration?

Employment policy. Have we kept employment policy and

standards adjusted to the dynamics of the economy, the labor market, and the conditions under which the work gets done? For example, are flexible work weeks and work days still an oddity not to be touched, or have they been tested and found sound or lacking where you work? Why were some organizations, including public service groups, so slow to make use of competent part-time help, such as well-educated housewives who are not available for full-time employment outside their homes?

Social environment. Are we influencing building design, construction and layout, procurement, legislation and public policy, government regulations, transportation, environmental and other social factors on behalf of the human element for which we claim primary responsibility?

This look at personnel administration through the eyes of top management should not end without some favorable comment, for there are some things for which I believe we deserve praise from on high. You may read these points as faint praise, but nevertheless, when management's expectations are met, they are met.

There are circumstances under which top management genuinely expects the personnel department to block a personnel action—for example, to find a candidate for employment or promotion unqualified, or to find a position substantively lacking in factors that would justify its upgrading for pay purposes. We doubtless look good in the eyes of top management when we apply our yardsticks and come out with the answer management wants. To do otherwise makes us an adversary of the hand that feeds us. And there are many personnel situations where the call can go either way.

Another area in which we shine is that of the paperwork management that attends all personnel offices. Admittedly, too many of us as personnel specialists continue to practice our art with a clerical mentality, but there are times when superb clerical work is needed in a personnel office. Top management is beset with many requirements for diverse data about its labor force. These requests originate both externally and internally, and the special requests are often urgent. In the larger organizations it takes computers and support personnel to assemble, analyze, and publish the data in readable form. An informed personnel specialist has to guide such efforts. In a small company it may take a good clerk and the personnel manager working late to get out the report, but it always does get out. We are pretty good at records, files, correspondence, and reports.

A third plus worth noting pertains to our capacity for survival and useful service during the ups and downs of the parent organization and its leadership. We are always on duty, like a funeral parlor, to take charge of the grim business of ushering out a regime. Likewise, we are always standing at attention on the doorstep of new leadership as it arrives. We help it get staffed up and moving. We honestly feel compassionate about those for whom it is time to go, and we earnestly seek to help new leaders as if they were infants. Our loyalty and dedication during such periods and whenever a crisis arises is unswerving and, in my judgment, truly commendable.

On balance, as I search for objective answers to the questions posed in this section and to related questions that might also be asked of ourselves, I'm afraid we get a barely passing score with top management. We may even be failing.

WHERE DO WE STAND WITH OPERATING OFFICIALS?

In the spring of 1978, the senior production official of a large 100-year-old manufacturing plant asked for my advice and help in connection with some major changes his plant was making in its customer relations and personnel assignments. I asked him how much help he had available from the personnel director and his staff. He shook his head and said, "Jim, the personnel director is a nice guy, but not too competent. He is a distant relative of the family holding a controlling interest in the company."

I met several times with the production man and his principal staff members. Not a single one of them ever mentioned the personnel department, and clearly they were out of touch with it even though their problems had implications across the board in all personnel functions. I wondered how long the gulf had existed, how wide it was, and whether or not it could ever be bridged. The plant was struggling to keep out of the red because of keen competition from other plants.

This item sparks in my mind another series of questions with which to confront ourselves in this critique.

Credibility. How much credibility do we have with operating officials on the basis of our total past performance and their knowledge of who we are, why we hold the positions we hold, and what we stand for? In a way, we are like a bank on a street corner. Our clients either have confidence in us and will cultivate a working relationship with us or they distrust us and will make other arrangements. Some banks tend to be very conservative in their policies, catering to other businesses instead of their individual depositors; others see a communitywide or even statewide responsibility, are willing to take a few risks, and seem to prosper more than the little bank that still prides itself in recognizing every depositor—and in making manual bookkeeping entries in pen and ink. I actually know a bank in each of these categories in the same metropolitan area. One has prospered, and the other hasn't.

Presence. What evidence is there that the personnel department has made special efforts to create a presence within the theater of operations? Has it remained aloof, resting on protocol and forcing operating officials to bear their burdens an extra mile, or has it moved in and set up camp where the problems are?

My experience is that the personnel people enjoy their collective security, operate out of relatively well-appointed offices in a central compound, and are not inclined to spend much time "on location."

Responsiveness. How responsive have we been to requests from operating officials for technical assistance? Have we been self-starting in giving the help we have given, or have operating officials had to cajole us into a commitment to lend a hand? Have we followed through in a businesslike way, or has our effort fizzled out? Do operating officials respect the contributions we make and consider them a full measure of our talents and abilities, or do you suspect that they regard our effort as too little too late?

I get a mixed result in judging us on this issue. Many of the personnel specialists I've known are truly dedicated people making every effort to please their client operating officials, and they go out of their way to do so. Others guard their jurisdictional borders and block the initiative of operating officials to try to do for themselves the kind of things they cannot seem to get the personnel department to do for them. For example, their efforts to recruit their own staff or develop their own employee training and development programs frequently are impeded by bureaucratic resistance in the personnel department.

Resource allocation. Have we allocated a reasonable share of our time and other resources to projects that might alleviate conditions seriously affecting the attainment of production goals? Why is turnover conspicuously higher in some departments than others? Accidents? Grievances? Customer complaints? Perhaps some job analysis and use of technology would reduce or eliminate the monotony in the affected jobs.

In my experience it is not so much a matter of resources as it is a problem of overcoming inertia to get started on problem solving for operating officials. There are many sources of free or inexpensive manpower—cooperative plan (work-study) universities, graduate students who need a research project, universities with a research grant, other in-house management groups, and even the operating department's own staff. All that is needed is a personnel specialist with some technical know-how, initiative, and ability to plan, organize, and direct a systematic study of the problem.

Delegation. Have we demonstrated sufficient confidence in operating officials to delegate a good measure of authority and responsibility to them for conducting their own internal personnel administration programs within a broad framework of policy we have established? This is the litmus test of how far we have come in developing an awareness and acceptance of the principles and processes of sound personnel administration.

Is it not true that sometimes we tend to single out an operating official, suspect every move he makes, withhold delegations of authority, monitor closely and carelessly speak of the official as if he were an outlaw? It is so easy to focus on a single move of an operating official, which may have been made in ignorance or in desperation. His fate may be hinged to that episode for years to come. Have we dealt justly and intelligently with the operating official who is on the firing line? I say we haven't.

Program balance. Are we neglecting any of our personnel functions, or is our program balanced and serving the total needs of our client operating officials? The personnel departments I've known were spotty in their capability and unbalanced in the coverage of their program responsibilities. They generally allocate the vast majority of their professional staff positions and dollars to employment and position classification. They make a token allocation to employee training and development, safety, and industrial relations. We are paying the price in goodwill lost as a result of this inequity, I believe.

Documentation. Have we managed the documentation of regulatory and procedural material pertaining to personnel administration to the operator's satisfaction? The charge that I hear is that either we publish a legalistic, complicated set of personnel regulations which others have difficulty understanding or we go to the other extreme and document very little. In the latter case, a few sporadic single-subject announcements may be made, but they eventually become obsolete and are seldom republished as a codified document. Generally, our writing lacks simplicity and readability.

I know an organization that has existed for 40 years without a manual of personnel policies, regulations, and procedures. The fragmentary body of policies it has are embedded in 40 years of minutes of its board of directors, which has revolving membership. The board's and the executive director's time is needlessly wasted on individual cases on which recorded policy is sketchy or silent.

Joint-venture planning. How often do we engage with operating officials in some joint-venture planning for the purpose of making future operations run smoother, and, in so doing, gain some personnel experience that may improve the state of the art? Are we doing any model building and pretesting of contemporary concepts on the operating scene? There are countless ways to reinforce existing methods of personnel supervision and management and to pilot alternative methods. How often do we take the initiative and make proposals to operating officials which are the result of completed staff work?

When we know that operating officials are planning to introduce a new product, service, or method, do we offer to develop a companion personnel program to facilitate the new venture? Specifically, the operations move may suggest some personnel initiatives such as selective recruitment, selection panels, training, new supervisors, or a promotion-from-within campaign.

Rewards and penalties. Operating officials are production-chart oriented. They are alert for upturns and downturns in the production curve. What are we as personnel specialists doing to build incentive systems that can spur production and generate rewards for outstanding producers? Also, to what extent are we supporting the operating official who wants to deal with marginal producers? The common complaint one hears in many organizations is that hours of duty and breaks are being abused and that many employees are not producing an acceptable day's work. Supervisors are forced to ignore the issue because they are fearful of finding themselves on the defensive in a grievance or court action. If these charges are true, and I believe they are, we are almost in the category of a co-conspirator.

Let us interrupt this interrogation again, from the angle of a group of our observers, and take note of some complimentary things to say about ourselves. It seems to me that there are a number of points we can credit ourselves with in our relationship with operating officials, and I believe most operating officials will concur.

One thing we can do pretty well is fill the lower-level jobs in operations. In private organizations with organized blue-collar labor, the union generally makes referrals. That still leaves clerks, typists, stenographers, messengers, and para-professionals such as draftsmen, lower-level computer personnel, bookkeepers, and the like. There is a revolving-door labor market for help of this kind, and I think we as a profession have to accept some responsibility for high turnover among these people. It is not hard to snare enough to keep vacancies filled. Most personnel offices have a small testing unit where applicants for clerical positions can be tested against the employer's standards. A few telephone calls will suffice to verify past employment and satisfy security and suitability requirements.

We can work out arrangements with, and supply information to, the payroll office to ensure that employees are paid on time. The payroll is taken as seriously as the earth's rhythms in its universe.

We can get out timely announcements of common interest to apprise employees of such items as top management appointments and losses, excused time off around holidays, employee benefit changes, reductions in force, and other matters.

We can publish a house organ year after year to record some of the more mundane happenings about the organization. While these newspapers and magazines vary in quality, they are as important to most employees as their daily newspaper and television news summary are. I am thinking of one official newspaper which was published by the personnel office for at least 20 years in essentially the same format. Employees regarded it so highly that they were sometimes seen snatching copies from handtrucks as the papers were wheeled in from the printer on payday.

Another blue star we can claim is for keeping an orderly system of central records and files. Personnel records and files are as critical to personnel administration as clinical records and charts are to medical people. We have thoroughly established the concept of a single, official file for every employee. The file can be charged out to anyone with a need to know; it is controlled; and the contents are monitored in accordance with predetermined standards for file maintenance. There are rules for its disposition when the employee leaves the organization. Much of the data in the file is summarized in manual or computerized data systems.

We have no difficulty in administering employee benefit packages, including leave, retirement, health insurance, Social Security, and others.

We can unravel the most complicated of personnel action cases. As I have indicated previously, we are case-oriented and seem to enjoy nothing more than digging into the chronological history of a chequered employment case to determine, for example, whether or not the individual is entitled to permanent status, retirement credit, or maximum vacation time.

Finally, we are not bad at organizing recreational opportunities for large numbers of employees. It may be an annual picnic, a winter bowling league, a summer tennis tournament, a garden club, or a hobby group in photography or duplicate bridge.

WHERE DO WE STAND WITH FOREMEN AND SUPERVISORS?

During a plane flight between New York and Washington, on the night of August 17, 1978, I became deeply engrossed in conversation with a young economist who was rushing to a southern city for a long hard weekend of work-related conferences. He is connected with a company dealing in the buying, processing, and selling of food commodities. The thrust of his message to me was that he is deeply concerned over the loss of the work ethic in the American economy. He didn't appear to be a workaholic but rather an individual who is fully committed to helping his company meet its objectives and continue to make a profit. He has some 300 employees under his general direction and is constantly having to concur in dismissal notices—essentially because employees at various levels of responsibility are not giving a day's work for a day's pay.

The first level of supervision and management is where the action is. Supervisors and foremen can make or break the best policy planning and executive leadership. Our standing as personnel specialists with these people should mean a great deal to us. Here are some self-examination questions.

Reference checks. How good are the reference checks we make with previous employers of job applicants? Typically, in my experience, the inquiry is from personnel clerk to personnel clerk. Questions are cursory, such as: "Is there anything derogatory in the person's file?" Since the real appraisal of an individual's past performance and potential is generally known only to former supervisors, peers, and subordinates, it is unlikely that the responding personnel clerk can be very helpful.

Representation. How courageously and attentively do we come to the defense of a supervisor or foreman when trouble erupts on the work scene? Assume the proposed action is a penalty action such as suspension from duty without pay, disapproval of an annual increment in pay, or separation for cause. The employee may countercharge discrimination and file a civil rights grievance. Do we sort out the facts and rise to the supervisor's defense whenever the circumstances merit it, or do we merely let the supervisor "stew in his own juice"? The first time we do the latter, you can be sure the word spreads.

Reserves during peak loads. In a military situation, there always seem to be sources of reserves that can be brought in to relieve hard-pressed troops. Do our personnel departments have any reserves on tap to relieve the supervisors who run our civilian armies of production and service? Why not?

There are countless people in every city "moonlighting" on second jobs they abhor. Why can't we develop a system for identifying qualified people for tasks they would enjoy doing on an on-call basis? For example, I know a school teacher who is a professional speech therapist. She moonlights in a department store as a sales clerk during the winter months to make extra money to pay her utility bills. Her school system could encourage the community to use the talents of such teachers by employing them as private tutors for children with special needs or exceptional abilities.

There must be possibilities, also, in reciprocity agreements among departments under which the employees of one department can work for another in slack periods and earn credits for the sending department which can be cashed in later as needed.

Alerts. How perceptive are we to the special needs of supervisors and foremen for advance information on changes that affect them? How often do we alert them to procedural changes and factors, such as ones that will affect transportation, lunch room service, space assignments, parking, and shifts?

Pay inequities. How objectively do we monitor the changes that are constantly made in job assignments from the standpoint of pay equity? We are prone to admonish supervisors to develop and utilize the fullest potential of each individual employee. Yet, when we see the supervisor doing some job enrichment and challenging an employee to new plateaus of performance, what do we do about it, besides giving the supervisor a hard time when he or she tries to make a case for promoting the employee? We are just as likely to see superannuated employees continually earning more and producing less. What have we done on our own initiative about these cases?

Collaboration. With whom do we collaborate, and why? Supervisors are aware of the company we keep with top management and operating officials. It is perhaps natural that we collaborate more at these levels than we do at the first level, because there are fewer bases to touch at the upper levels. However, I am afraid that supervisors suspect us of unfriendly collaboration against their best interests. We need to relate to and communicate more directly with supervisors to gain their confidence.

It seems to me that we measure up about the same in the eyes of foremen and supervisors as we do in the sight of operating officials. They recognize certain strengths, and they count on those to continue. I seriously doubt that they ever expect us to overcome the weaknesses just noted.

WHERE DO WE STAND WITH EMPLOYEES?

On August 22, 1978, I had a conversation with a construction superintendent of a nationwide company about labor–management relations in his company. He revealed that his company is almost totally dependent on unions for manpower. The company's personnel office takes very little initiative, having no recruitment program, no training program even for foremen, and no performance standards. And yet his company specializes in putting up buildings, such as shopping centers and commercial office buildings, where the owners want them in place fast. The company apparently hires and fires people as fast as they can throw brick and mortar in place. They have also learned the lesson of how to bribe state and local government officials and suppliers in certain states for needed cooperation.

He stated that some of the firm's superintendents and general foremen have little or no ability to delegate, and when they are not on the job, production practically stops. He also noted communication failures in his company. In his long career in the industry, the superintendent has been impressed with the fact that some companies have a knack for motivating their employees and others do not.

We are agents of management, and employees know it. Therefore, we have to make extraordinary efforts to win the confidence and respect of employees. I would not want our pay and future to depend on employees' appraisal of our performance as an arm of management. Here are some of the reasons.

Pressures. Do we resist the pressures to distort sound personnel administration? In my experience, we are not very successful at resisting the many pressures that tend to bend our will and lead to our becoming a party to position classification and pay inequities, violation of qualification standards in employment and promotion actions, and assorted kinds of discrimination and favoritism, nepotism, and do-nothingness at times when courage is required.

Secrecy. Do we operate the personnel system in an atmosphere of openness, or do we cloak it with mystery and intrigue? It is a well-known fact that organizations bound by published ground rules for reduction in force, in anticipation of such a move, do dry runs to see who will be hit. If some untouchables are hit in the dry run, the whole maneuver is redesigned and tested under a modified set of criteria, and this mock exercise is repeated until the personnel office in collaboration with operating officials and top management is satisfied that the outcome will be as they wish it to be.

The business of having pay distributed in sealed envelopes so that no employee will presumably know what other employees are paid has always struck me as secrecy of the worst kind. There are few if any secrets about pay. This facade is not helping our image. I know of an organization which has for years published promotions and annual salary rates in its monthly house organ. Mayors and city managers in Northern Virginia were forced by public pressure generated by a suburban newspaper to publish the salaries of all employees whose annual rate exceeded a certain rate. Consequently,

Fairfax County, Virginia, reported 738 county employees making more than $20,000 and 522 of its top public school employees making more than $25,000. About the same time, Northwest Orient Airlines, in a battle with the pilots' union, bought a full-page ad in at least one metropolitan newspaper to list the salaries of its pilots. They reported that a Northwest 747 captain made $105,739 in 1977 (W-2 earnings of $83,080, pension funding of $21,684, life insurance of $312, and medical/dental insurance of $663); and that 302 of its pilots earned more than a U.S. senator. They were objecting publicly to pilots not accepting $30,000 in wage and benefits raises over three years. These are all examples of how openness with salary data can serve the public interest.

Incentives and promotion opportunities. Do we lay on the line adequate incentives and promotion opportunities to attract and hold capable people? I once worked for an organization with a large professional staff of architects and engineers. It had let the staff age seriously by contracting work out instead of introducing new blood at the junior and journeyman levels. An attitude of futility in competing in the industry pervaded the organization. However, once it explored the possibilities of an accelerated training and promotion agreement, starting pay became a secondary consideration for young college graduates. It soon became clear that they were more interested in the incentive of a continuing growth program and a scheduled promotion plan subject to up or out action.

Leveling. Are we forthright with employees as to whose interests we are there to protect, or do we try to get the employee to believe that we are safeguarding him? If the answer to this question favored employees, union membership would probably decline drastically. We can't level. We hold back some of the information we have when we communicate with the employee, and he knows it. For example, we play the game of posting selected job vacancies when we and many of the interested employees know we have no intention of filling the vacancy from the responses.

Separations. What is our batting average with respect to overseeing the departure of employees from a long and generally successful career with our organizations? Is it not true that many of our most outstanding employees remain at their posts until they stagnate, and that during their last few years they are shunted about in "special assistant to" roles and arduous field assignments to induce retirement? I have seen individuals who were no longer wanted in executive ranks intimidated, humiliated, and harassed because they were not willing to step aside for younger staff or people whom a new regime wanted to bring aboard.

This predatory, jungle-like practice is widespread. To the extent that our personnel offices condone these practices, we are co-conspirators in a shameful activity. It can soon bankrupt an organization's goodwill account as people take their leave of the place and settle into retirement or second careers. We need a system for dealing more humanely with people during the twilight of their first career so that they may depart with grace and their self-respect intact.

It is hard to know what good points employees see in us, since they are so different in their hopes and aspirations. Sooner or later we may do something pleasing for a particular employee, but almost inevitably that is negated by another move we make. Perhaps we are in a sense to employees like the office of the prison warden is to the inmates. We provide central services—mail, records, special benefits—and a central focus for any individual in the system who wants to have a special problem adjudicated. Such an office can't be all bad, but it can never win massive acclaim, since it must function within a disciplined atmosphere and uphold a work ethic that is anathema to many people.

WHERE DO WE STAND WITH PEOPLE LOOKING FOR WORK?

We must not leave this critique without examining our performance through the eyes of individuals on the outside who are looking for work and will soon gain their first impression of life inside our organization. Since first impressions can endure for many years, whether the job applicant gets the job or not, it is especially important that we get off to a good start with each person who approaches us at the reception counter or by telephone or the written word. Here are some more questions.

Currency. How current are our front-line representatives on organizational relationships, product lines and services, job requirements, pending vacancies, wages and benefits, career development opportunities, and labor–management contract terms? Do these representatives speak with understanding and enthusiasm on matters which the applicants ask questions about? Do our responses by phone and mail convey the best tone and pitch? Too often, I'm afraid, our spokespeople have to sign off with the forlorn statement, "We will hold your application in our files and let you know if anything opens up for which you can qualify." They simply are not current on the manpower needs, present or pending, in the organization areas they are expected to serve.

Dialog. Do our employment interviewers use finesse, good taste, and objectivity in framing the questions they put to job applicants? Are they good listeners, or do they do most of the talking? Do they prepare for the interview by studying the application and ferreting out questions that will amplify or gather key information? Unfortunately, we all think we are better than we are at picking people on the basis of an interview. Our interviewers sometimes ask discriminatory questions. Some of us ask young married women, "What are your plans for having a family?" And we ask mothers, "How do you manage your child care problem?"

Expectations. Do we make it clear from the outset what the vacancy picture is and what the qualification standards are? Do we refer job applicants to the right people in operations, where the selections are made, or merely to another receptionist there? Do we let the candidate wait for an answer interminably at the employment office and for weeks or months when he or she has returned home? These are but a few ways in which we build false expectations in job applicants. Whether the applicant gets the job he wants or not, the treatment detracts from our image.

There are two pluses we can probably collect from the person looking for work. First, we are unbeatable at selecting a young, attractive, shapely, and friendly female receptionist to station at the front desk in the employment office. She may be totally uninformed as to how the machinations of the personnel system work, but she is there with her smile to greet the walk-ins. She anesthetizes the applicant.

Second, we usually manage to get the space in which the receptionist works spruced up and made as inviting as she is. Except for the personnel director, she has the classiest quarters in the personnel department, and this is as it should be, I believe.

WHERE DO WE STAND IN OUR OWN EYES AS PERSONNEL SPECIALISTS?

The value of our contributions in personnel administration in the eyes of others who are in a position to observe us may not be nearly as important as our self-assessment of our worth to the organization. If we are bringing an adequate amount of specialized knowledge, skill, and ability to the work, with conviction and perseverance, nothing else much matters. I have these questions for us.

Identity. Do we have a clear, constant understanding of whom we in the personnel office should serve, or do we behave pragmatically, taking first a position favorable to management and later wavering to support the employee? My experience is that we have identity problems and our behavior pattern is unpredictable.

Layering. Are we unfettered, with the widest possible latitude for independent action, or do we have to operate within the guidelines established by a too-tall hierarchy above the personnel director? The fact is that we are layered and restricted. For example, dismissals for cause in operating departments are usually subject to appeal to the chief executive or to an appeals board created by him—not to the personnel director or chief of employment.

Sparkle. Do we have class and sparkle? Or does our eclipsed place in top management's sun, our lack of first-rate leadership, the degree to which we have been bent to management's will, our drab and isolated physical facilities, our confused identity and other qualities alluded to above combine to present us as a colorless team? There are too many erosive conditions to keep our image sparkling, although I believe there are instances when we come on like a bright light in the sky. For example, I have known personnel offices to show tremendous compassion and helpfulness during a tragic episode in an employee's life or that of a loved one.

Voice. Does our personnel director have a seat in the "cabinet" of the chief executive, with an active voice in the major decisions, or does he have to play a subordinate role like a page boy or girl in political chambers? The latter is generally closer to the truth.

Extra baggage. To what extent are we used as "donkeys" to handle extra baggage that doesn't belong in the personnel department? How many of our legitimate functions have slid into other management areas? Too often, we lack a discrete set of functions.

Creativity. How much rein do we have for being creative, using research and development methods? Are we regarded as a "ferry boat crew," there to get people to where they are going, or do others look to us to play a role in the improvement of the "transportation system"? I had the privilege of knowing the late Floyd Shannon, whose career was with the Western Electric Company of AT&T. He was intimately involved in the kind of behavioral science research that went on in its Hawthorne plant in the 1930s, and he had a hand in the development of its fine executive development center in New Jersey. Mr. Shannon was no ferry boat operator!

Now for the other side of the coin. We see plenty of possibility in personnel administration, or most of us would not have stuck with it as long as we have. We still have high hopes for its recognition and full support by top management.

We are dedicated to continue the practice of personnel administration to the best of our ability. We will continue the search for the best talent available with which to staff organizations, and keep our commitment to the fullest development and utilization of the potentials of each individual, regardless of race, creed, color, national origin, sex, marital status, political persuasion, or other extraneous factors.

Our career in personnel administration is, or was, on the whole most gratifying. We can point to enough good we've done to more than offset the negative impressions we have of ourselves and others may have of us. Still, we know full well that things are not as they should be, and we are open to suggestions for improvement. We want to make our work more fulfilling as we try to find better ways to make it more nearly meet the expectations of top management, operating officials, foremen and supervisors, employees, and persons looking for work.

Chapter 2

The Roots of Our Problems

WHAT DO YOU see as possible root causes of the conditions outlined in Chapter 1? Knowing the historical causes should, of course, simplify the search for solutions. Therefore, this chapter presents an array of specific causes that appear to be contributing factors.

Obviously, not all of these factors plague every personnel office, and by no means do they deserve equal weight. The material is intended more as a checklist of factors to use in critically examining the performance of your central personnel department and its local branches. They can be grouped under six headings:

1. Top management posture.
2. Deficiencies in leadership.

3. Program planning deficiencies.
4. Communication gaps.
5. Stunted professional growth.
6. Weak personnel management.

TOP MANAGEMENT POSTURE

In contract law, the principal is responsible for the acts of his agents. This concept fits well in the relationship between top management and the personnel department.

Distorted Value System

Some managements make little or no commitment to the development and maximum utilization of their human resources. In this thinking, economic growth and development and net profits overshadow all other management considerations. Such managements have not learned that good management and economic objectives are more easily realized through careful selection and development of people than by using people as if they were expendable hand tools and supplies. They may see compliance with the minimum-wages and maximum-hours laws as the limit of their obligation to the people who produce and deliver the goods and services. Value distortions of this kind will inevitably control the scope and quality of the personnel program.

Loose Conglomerates

As organizations grow, decentralize, and merge with others into conglomerates, the ability to sustain a cohesive and coherent personnel program is severely tested. I am thinking, for instance, of a nationwide organization with some 30,000 employees. It was constituted about 1950 by consolidating five independent organizations with distantly related services. Nearly three decades later, it still has not amalgamated the loose conglomeration and fully coordinated the personnel services across the board. The concept of a single employer is not practiced, even though many of the professional skills are transferable.

Excessive Demands and Abuses

Some managements make excessive demands on their personnel departments, and they can become abusive when such demands get no response or a slow response. For example, consider the case of an employee who takes a stand in a community action program. The matter may come to the attention of a senior executive who finds it in conflict with his own position on the issue. The executive insists that the employee be summarily fired by the personnel department. The employee's folder may have several letters of commendation and reflect nothing but outstanding service over a sustained period of years. Earlier, the same organization may even have proclaimed a policy of encouraging its staff to take an active part in community life where they live.

Nonparticipative Management

The same managements which are quick to impose unreasonable demands on their personnel departments are often slow to lend an ear to their voice when new directions, policies, and programs are being formulated. Participative management is not a process that works exclusively at the lower levels of supervision and management. The personnel department could benefit from practicing it in its relationship with top management. The personnel staff should not be in the position of having to administer large-scale personnel programs for operating departments to support operating programs they were not privileged to discuss in the conceptual planning stages.

DEFICIENCIES IN LEADERSHIP

The effectiveness of any program is influenced by the caliber of the top leaders who are directing the planning and administration of the program. It is my deep conviction that there are conspicuous shortcomings in the qualifications and performance of people assigned to leadership roles in many personnel departments. Several specific reasons for this are discussed below.

Sparse Sources of Supply

The older, more recognized professions, such as medicine, law, science, and engineering, have established institutions of learning that systematically develop high-potential young people who are capable of becoming practitioners with some on-the-job training and practical work experience. In personnel administration, such institutions are few and far between. I know of no college or university with a school of personnel administration.

Individuals who enter this field in many cases have no preparation beyond high school, other than practical experience. Others have college-level background in such fields as education, sociology, political science, public administration, business administration, or industrial relations. The chances are remote that the practitioner has had as much relevant formal education as do physicians, attorneys, scientists, engineers, or any of numerous other professional practitioners. In fact, it is likely that the personnel director's household pet is seen by a veterinarian with substantially more professional training than the director himself has had for his dealings with human beings at work.

Lack of Coherence

Since the personnel director as a young person generally does not set his sights on personnel administration as a profession and school himself for years to prepare for a lifelong career in it, we tend to get short-termers in the personnel director's chair. The personnel director in many cases is the product of work in a narrow specialty in personnel administration, such as position classification or employment; he is not well grounded in all aspects of a comprehensive human resources program. Neither is he grounded in one or more of the substantive fields of the parent organization's mission. In other instances, the personnel director may be a "transient" on his way to retirement or to an upper echelon management position, with the personnel job serving as an interim assignment until an appropriate vacancy or new position can be created. This lack of an orderly system for producing candidates for the personnel director post makes for less stability and coherence in the personnel program.

Wellsprings for Union Strength

Union members and their leaders can easily sense weaknesses in the opposition camp. The situation is analogous to a professional sports team which is prone to frequent and abrupt changes in the coaching staff. The program has not been shored up and supported over a period of years against the erosive effects of grievances and personnel service failures. Good staff work has not been done to match the staff work done by union leaders. Communication between personnel leaders and union leaders has been cumbersome and sporadic. Tempers have been volcanic on both sides.

Failures to Resist Pressures to Prostitute Standards

Personnel directors and their senior staff have too often been a part of the problem instead of a wall of stubborn resistance to wreckage of professional personnel standards. The hiring of any unqualified person above the unskilled-laborer or routine-clerical level can do irreparable damage to operations objectives. The promotion of an unqualified person over the heads of qualified persons can ravage morale. Failures to settle grievances promptly and judiciously can aggravate labor–management relations. Condoning of discriminatory practices can open the floodgates of pressure groups against the organization. These and other examples of failures to resist encroachments on professional standards long ago convinced me of the absolute necessity for personnel department leadership to be unwavering in its resistance effort.

PROGRAM PLANNING DEFICIENCIES

Very few personnel departments have anything resembling a long-range planning capability. Planning, if done at all, is considered an integral part of the responsibility of each senior staff member. This deficiency is reflected in ways such as the following.

Failure to Provide Common-Need Services of High Quality

A health unit is often one of the services provided by the personnel department. Such a unit can save untold lost production time and contribute to the employees' general health and state of mind. It must be conveniently located, competently staffed, and efficiently managed.

The lunch room and vending machines are other services that are commonly overseen by the personnel department. Nothing can be more depressing than a drab, poorly appointed lunch room with unpleasant odors and noises. The uninviting environment is often accompanied by unappetizing food. Conditions of this sort force employees to start "brown-bagging" for lunch or leaving the building in search of outside eating places. Since employees generally have to use more time for lunch and breaks when they go outside their building, production and the personnel department are the losers.

There are a variety of other services the personnel department should conceptually plan and administer effectively. These are discussed in Chapter 5.

Mistakes in Judgment

Having too little planning capability, our personnel departments tend to be on a hand-to-mouth basis in the implementation of personnel services. We are driven by crises, each of which ostensibly differs from all the others we have faced. It seems to me that we strike out on a lot of these crises when we face them alone. We make too little use of multiple judgment as a problem-solving technique. And we fail dismally when we do not log and do a post-mortem on the development of each major program and on the evolution of each crisis. In brief, we are not good historians and archival managers, and this defect in work habits makes us susceptible to mistakes in judgment.

Not Keeping Pace

Operating officials are always on the move. They know that to stand still is to fall behind on their production and service goals. And this is where we as personnel specialists sometimes miss golden opportunities. We let production people get far in front of us in planning new ventures.

I am deeply committed to the proposition that personnel specialists have to go joint-venture with operating people. For every step the operator takes we must take a parallel step which will ensure that the human resources will be in place and capable of performing proficiently when a new phase of production begins. All personnel processes or only selected ones may be required. Therefore, a personnel team or task group or only an individual member of the staff may be needed. We have to be a part of the action and keep pace with operating people.

Lack of Dialog with Reform Groups

We have kept a "duck and cover" posture with respect to reform groups that pressed for reform of personnel practice. Of course, it is not very easy to convince top management of a single establishment that it should introduce reforms in a whole industry or branch of the public service. However, professional societies are presumably interested in moving their profession and its members to higher levels of service. What have we done through our professional societies to bring about major reforms? Here is a partial list of reforms that have been won by outside special interest groups working through legislative bodies and political administrations.

Veterans preference. In 1978 both houses of the Congress of the United States overwhelmingly rejected President Carter's proposal to cut back veterans' absolute preference in hiring and firing practices of the federal government. The Veterans Preference Act of 1944 has held against all efforts to weaken it. This act, in my judgment, gives protection far too long during the working career of the veteran and contributes to inefficiency in government—a condition that critics of federal government say they want to eliminate.

Civil service reform groups. Groups such as the National Civil Service Reform League and the International Personnel Management Association have pressed to have larger percentages of civil servants blanketed under the merit systems of federal, state, and local governments.

Labor unions. Unions have fought vigorously for higher pay and fringe benefits, shorter hours, ironclad guarantees against reductions in the labor force, better working conditions, and other benefits.

Civil rights activists. There is no question as to where the civil rights movement began. Underprivileged and oppressed minorities and their spiritual and political leaders began a drumbeat in the South, which gathered momentum until such milestones as the public school desegregation case of 1954 and the Civil Rights Act of 1963 were won. To the best of my knowledge, none of this drumbeat came from our personnel offices or our personnel administration societies. Why not? Why did we take no initiative in this struggle and remain aloof after it began? What is our mood on the matter today? Are we dragging our feet and letting employees take us to court, or do we search out pockets of noncompliance and act decisively?

Women. Prohibition of discrimination against people because of their sex was inserted as an afterthought in the Civil Rights Act of 1963. In the 1970s, women have worked to try to get the Equal Rights Amendment (ERA) ratified by two-thirds of the state legislatures, but they still lack three states and there is talk of some of the ratifying states reversing their stand. Yet, personnel statistics dramatically portray the underrepresentation of women in executive positions in American business, industry, and government. Where were we personnel specialists and our societies in this reform movement?

Equal employment opportunity (EEO) and affirmative action programs. We can treat civil rights philosophically, settle into a state of indifference, and rationalize that it is a political hot potato that is too hot for us to handle. In the meantime, there is the practical matter of bringing about some change in a predominantly white labor force and a predominantly male staff of supervisors and managers.

What about our responsibility to bring about more equal employment opportunity through affirmative action (that is, a better balance in the employee mix)? We can let department heads hide behind the facade of "we would be glad to take some blacks or Mexican-Americans, but we can find no qualified applicants in those categories." Another option would be for us to run an aggressive, imaginative recruitment campaign, an intensive in-service training program, or a promotion-from-within system to get some upward mobility of dead-ended individuals already on the payroll. We can also comply more with the federally funded Comprehensive Employment and Training Act (CETA), which aims to provide individuals with marketable skills and guide them into an employment situation where they can sustain themselves.

Physically handicapped special interest groups. It was my good fortune once to have employed two deaf and mute statistical typists. They soon became the most productive statistical typists in the history of the organization, because they were not affected by noise distractions and they simply tried harder to achieve than normal statistical typists. I have heard of a blind person with a stick who independently negotiates the longest subway escalator in the world on her way to and from work. Numerous other examples could be given to illustrate the point that physically handicapped persons should not be passed over in hiring. Where were we as personnel specialists when the emphasis on hiring the physically handicapped began?

Mentally retarded. The uninitiated in the use of mentally retarded people are likely to reject the notion outright without batting an eye. You might be making a serious mistake to do so. I know a mentally retarded person who has been employed for over a decade in a large printing and distribution plant. She gets commendations and incremental raises in pay and has a large following of customers who rely on her to get out their work efficiently.

Prisoner rehabilitation cases. Another category of people in the potential labor force which has been easy for us to turn our backs on is that of the individual who has served (or is still serving) a prison term. It is so easy for the first offense to close the door permanently on employment opportunities. People with prison records may have obtained a marketable skill through job training and counseling services during their prison term, but they have to get the first job and succeed on it to have anything to build on. The personnel office can make or break such an individual. Are we doing enough in this area?

Older persons. Again, we seem to have left the reforms in the use of the knowledge, skills, and abilities of older persons to special interest groups such as the American Association for Retired People and the Retired Teachers Association. The common practice of forcing workers to retire at 65 became illegal under an April 1978 amendment of the Age Discrimination in Employment Act. By a lop-sided vote, Congress made it unlawful to forcibly retire most nonmilitary federal workers at any age and most other public or private workers under age 70.

Special interest groups for older persons are constantly winning new reforms for their members through court action and legislation. They also press local governments and commercial interests into giving their members discounts and special benefits which save them money and make life more comfortable. Where were we as personnel specialists in this movement? It seems to me that we could, if we were so inclined, interpret our role as one that follows the employee into retirement. It would be good business to do so.

COMMUNICATION GAPS

The personnel office is somewhat like a lost battalion. Enmeshed in a tangle of cases, it fights on, but without the advantages of effective communication. Apart from the gap with reform groups, discussed in the preceding section, I see a number of serious communication gaps.

Communication Gaps with Client Groups

Since we are not, in my view, accepted as a senior partner of top management, we are not privileged to enjoy the confidences and total support of the upper echelons of leadership. This leaves us out of touch and out of step at times with the chief executive and his staff.

For reasons already alluded to, we also have some difficulties dealing harmoniously and productively with operating officials, foremen and supervisors, employees generally, and persons looking for work. I believe the communication gaps are not due to technical difficulties with the telephone, the intercom, or messenger and mail systems. They stem from more fundamental problems. We haven't established the proper liaison. We haven't spent enough time away from our bureaucratic desks doing meaningful job analysis, following up on placements, inquiring into grievance and turnover causes, helping to plan career development and job training programs, advising on incentive possibilities, and the like.

These comments are not intended as a blanket condemnation of our communications. Parts of it excel. Many of our house organs have tremendous value. Some of us have succeeded in making bulletin boards useful, especially where a single message is attractively framed at conspicuous locations. Employee handbooks sometimes hit the mark, especially when they are interspersed with some good cartoons that help the personnel office and employees alike laugh at themselves.

Communication Gaps with Labor Groups and Other Employee Organizations

Some kind of reasoning has led us to regard labor groups as enemy camps. I wonder whether we shy away from free communication with labor because we sense that top management frowns on the practice and would regard us as unfaithful collaborationists. Once when I was planning a staff college and was moved to confer with the labor camp to gather any suggestions it had, I was told in no uncertain terms by a senior executive to forget the thought. It wasn't easy to forget, and I still believe management was wrong.

There are many facets of personnel administration on which I believe we could have a useful dialog with labor leaders. These include working conditions, employee benefits, personnel procedures, orientation of new employees, supervisor training, recreational opportunities, common-need services, facilities planning, incentive plans, performance appraisal, morale, and work simplification.

Communication Gaps with the Community at Large

It was my misfortune within the span of a month to lose two former professional associates, one to heart disease and one to cancer. Before and after the memorial services held in their honor, I found clusters of retired people who had worked with the deceased having a quiet but joyful reunion in the church vestibule. It obviously was the only occasion most of them had had to see each other for a long time, and it was pathetic that it took death to bring them together. Within three miles of the two churches stands the headquarters building of the organization for which several dozen retired citizens worked—some of them for 30 years or more. It would cost a pittance for that organization to sponsor a reunion with light refreshments or a bring-your-own-basket picnic in the park. The advantages of stable communication bridges to the community are too numerous to enumerate.

STUNTED PROFESSIONAL GROWTH

The scope and sophistication of some professions, such as electronics and computer science, have grown by leaps and bounds. Personnel administration has taken about four or five decades to grow and mature as much as computer science grew in a tenth of the time. I attribute this stunted growth to three major factors: the nonprofessional status of personnel administration, its confused identity, and lack of discretion.

Personnel as a Nonprofessional Art

It was not until 1883 that the Congress of the United States saw fit to enact legislation establishing a merit system and the U.S. Civil Service Commission. It took the assassination of a president (Garfield) to precipitate that action. The term personnel as we know it today appeared in the language of a report by the U.S. Civil Service Commission in 1909. The Secretary of Commerce and Labor followed in 1910 by using the term in his report. However, it was 1939 before the practice of personnel administration in the federal civil service enjoyed enough support in the executive branch of the federal government to merit an executive order establishing the post of director of personnel.

In contrast, within ten years after the introduction of the first computer in about 1950, a whole hierarchy of computer industry positions was widely in use. The relative pace for developing personnel administration in state and local government and the private sector appears to me to have been about the same as in the federal civil service. Prior to 1939 in the federal government, personnel functions were regarded as a better grade of clerical work which just about anyone could master in a short time. Personnel offices now have complex qualification standards for professional personnel positions. They seek candidates from such academic disciplines as sociology, education, psychology, industrial relations, business administration, public administration, and anthropology.

Confused Identity

As personnel people we have had mixed emotions about the work we do. Some of us become emotionally involved in cases, letting our judgment and our commitment to do top management's will be compromised by our emotional distress over the consequences of a penalty action against an employee. For example, suppose you are given the task of developing the case for firing an employee because of chronic alcoholism which has seriously affected his productivity over a period of several years. You find on investigation that the employee's credit is overextended, the marriage is in trouble, and the children are in need of parental attention. Do you compound the employee's troubles by terminating employment, thereby deeply jeopardizing his chances of landing a new job?

An exhaustive investigation into why the employee became an alcoholic in the first place might reveal that your employer was the real culprit. It could be a case of not having kept the individual updated in his field, having passed him over for a fully deserved promotion, or having underutilized his highest skills. Management's order to develop the case for firing stands. We are left with the same inside feelings an executioner must have in a capital punishment case. And, unfortunately, the personnel specialist who gets the case is not the only member of the staff who has an identity crisis. Under the circumstances cited, the hands of specialists throughout the personnel office would not be clean. Any of them might have saved the individual from the crisis by acting with more initiative and professional expertise.

Lack of Discretion

When we have an identity crisis in cases such as the one just hypothesized, we tend to talk about them to anyone who will listen. A Spanish proverb says: "Whoever gossips to you will gossip about you." The first rule in personnel administration is to remain absolutely discreet on what we know about individual employees and to conduct our investigations with strict confidentiality.

As we confide in selected employees about the fate or good fortune of other employees, we lower the confidants' appraisal of us and do irreparable damage to the affected employees. It is in as poor taste as it would be for a physician to discuss by name the physical condition of certain patients with other patients. This tendency on our part not to treat our case work with the same discretion as attorneys and physicians has damaged our image and slowed our growth as a profession.

WEAK PERSONNEL MANAGEMENT

Although personnel administration is a member of the modern management family, we are not known as a showcase of modern management. Several areas in which we often fall short are discussed below.

Failure to Innovate

Our procedures are woefully lacking in imagination. For example, many of us are still in the rut of offering orientation to the new employee as a part of the entrance upon duty routine. This is far from the best time to orient a new employee. The employee is ill at ease in a new environment and with people with whom he is not acquainted. His primary concerns on the first day are more likely to meet his supervisor, find his work place, get settled, and try to accomplish something that will gain his supervisor's approval. Orientation might well be introduced in self-instructional, learner-pacing format, using technology that would enable the new employee to check out a small audio-visual device for home use. Thus, the orientation could be spaced, on off-the-clock time, and of value to other interested members of the new employee's family.

Complacency about Space and Facilities

We are inclined to prepare for the coming of the customer to our commerical establishment or the citizen to our public service offices as if they were members of a royal family. For example, it is not uncommon in modern shopping centers to find spacious, air-conditioned malls in which one can enjoy beautiful arrangements of greenery, lighting, music, lounge furniture, and displays. Perhaps some exotic birds and interesting animals are added attractions.

In the executive offices of the same large shopping center, there is a personnel office that does the hiring of people and the contracting for services needed to design, decorate, repair, and maintain the mall space. The personnel space may be marginally decorated, congested, uncomfortable in weather extremes, and far below the standard of the public areas in the mall nearby. I know a restaurant owner who has the skimpiest rest rooms imaginable. His attitude is that rest rooms make him no profit, so why spend any unnecessary dollars on them? These same rest rooms are intended for the use of his employees, who constantly complain among themselves about the facilities.

Inadequate Staff Work

One of the finest management concepts ever developed is that of "completed staff work." We are not good at completed staff work in personnel administration. Instead, we are addicted to the use of "buck slips" on which we scribble a few words of comment or a question or two and shuttle the case on to another desk. I once knew someone who wrote nothing at all on his buck slips except one or more question marks. The severity of his concern about a case could be measured exactly by the number of giant question marks he emblazoned on the slip with a very soft lead pencil.

Completed staff work need not be an exhaustive document. It can be done in a page or less, using three or four headings such as: the problem, discussion of options, and action recommendation. It needs a line on which the reviewer or decision maker can indicate approval or disapproval.

Another area in which we could improve our staff work is in preparing for labor–management negotiations. Here is where good staff work can make a substantial difference in the final settlement, and the final settlement can have far-reaching effects for years to come in productivity, morale, turnover, and net profits.

Hostility Toward Sister Functions

We fight with our allies and dissipate our time for creativity. In my experience, the management family is like a family of quarreling children—jealous, suspicious, uncooperative, and uncompromising. Financial management and personnel administration are two of the worst antagonists. The holder of the purse strings wants absolute control over every penny of expenditures and encumbrances. For example, a promotion or job reclassification increases costs, and therefore the financial office wants to give prior approval to such personnel actions. Personnel people find the rigidity of financial control hard to understand. They want control through staffing ceilings and position classification.

I believe none of the issues that separate the antagonists is so serious that it could not be resolved on friendly terms. The financial office could make quarterly allotments to a reserve account to cover a limited number of promotions, and monitor the account from information copies of official personnel actions. The same procedure could be used to fund an employee training and development account from which tuition and fees for outside courses are paid.

Failure to Resolve Internal Problems

With one exception, the personnel offices I have known well were not examples of model personnel administration. They were like the proverbial shoemaker's children who are known for their threadbare shoes. None of the personnel offices in my experience was established from scratch during the period in which I observed them, but this hardly excuses them from practicing the highest state of the art in filling vacancies; separating incompetent employees; staff development and utilization; the use of standards of performance, incentives, and recognition to stimulate productivity and morale; the administration of equitable position classification and compensation systems; or the prompt and just settlement of grievances.

Most of these personnel offices procrastinated about solving their internal problems. In part, the delays were due to the pressure to solve their clients' personnel problems; to make a change would mean a slowdown in the projects on which the employees in question were presumably getting some work done. It is analogous to changing firefighters while fighting a fire.

These same personnel offices did not deal with their superannuated employee problems any better than nonpersonnel organizations did. They did not anticipate their vacancies and do an intelligent job of positive recruitment and cautious selection. They did not use their professional counseling capability to alleviate complex human relations problems in their back room.

Failure to Use Realistic Systems of Performance Appraisal

Of all the concepts advocated by personnel specialists, my candidate for the lowest failing mark is performance appraisal. Again, the track record of the personnel offices I have known is no better and no worse than that of non-personnel groups. There is something fundamentally wrong about the way we attempt to apply the principle, which is still sound conceptually.

Consumerism has come a long way in appraising products and services in the marketplace. Ralph Nader is still around, and countless others have joined him in his campaign to get a fair deal for the consumer. Why do we behave so poorly in judging the performance of human beings?

I believe there are several factors. We seldom set standards of performance in advance of a rating period and in partnership with the employee rated. We usually try to keep the evaluation on a one-to-one basis, which puts us in the role of judging another human being. Human compassion impedes us from giving a harsh rating even when it is deserved. We also fear the consequences of its being done to us, perhaps by a friend of the one we rate harshly.

We use a form that is complicated and demands summarizing in subjective adjectives, numbers, categories, or relative standings. We cannot bring ourselves to talk the rating over honestly in a face-to-face interview. We are not willing to document the employee's file during the rating period to support a realistic rating. We shrink from the possibility of a hearing in which we may have to defend a penalty rating.

Failure to Streamline Functionally

We have been carrying some "extra baggage" in the personnel office for years. I have long advocated that the employee training and development function be separated out from personnel. It will never get the funding, staffing, and support from the personnel leadership it needs. Moreover, the regulatory and disciplinary nature of some of the legitimate work of the personnel office will always detract from the constructive work that staff development specialists are interested in doing.

Safety seems to me another function that is misplaced in the personnel office. Safety needs to be under the wing of an engineer, and engineers are out of place in the personnel office. Most organizations have a buildings management function or a chief engineer. Safety could repose with such groups and perhaps get an assist from the employee training and development function. These are only two examples. Chapter 3 is more definitive on this point.

Absence of Real Quality Control

The work of assembly lines is reinforced by inspectors who are positioned at strategic points to check on the progress of the product as it is made. We all are used to opening packages in which a slip drops out reading, "Inspected by Inspector No. ______." This, I suppose, is a way of having the consumer inspect the work of the inspector. If, say, Inspector No. 35 is guilty of letting a shirt get past him with a flaw in it and the customer takes the shirt back, Inspector No. 35 may be called to account and could eventually find himself back on the line.

In the personnel office, we have no "Inspector No. 35." The work is done by individuals who might as well be working in watertight compartments on a ship. Little or no review occurs. For example, I've never known of a job to be re-audited by a second desk auditor. Individual specialists enjoy a degree of "sovereignty" that employees in many lines of work lack. There is no independent body, such as a board of visitors in academe or bank examiners in the banking world, making systematic inspections to determine the quality of decisions and the currency of the theory and practice used. The only brake on personnel administration is the system of internal and external pressures and complaints. Unfortunately, this system does not uniformly bring to the surface all instances of malpractice.

Henry Ford II told a Grosse Pointe, Michigan, "Crisis Club" in the fall of 1978: "America can't afford to sell mediocrity to the world." He said we need to get back standards of quality, not only in products, but in "speaking honestly, dealing honorably, and giving full value as promised." This is a concise summary of what this chapter is all about.

Chapter 3

Implications of Continuing on Our Present Course

ONE OPTION when an organization, system, or method is not working as well as it should is to do nothing. Many are prone to do just that in connection with personnel administration. In their view, the situation is analogous to a beehive of ailing but potentially hostile bees: it is much easier to walk around it and ignore it than to clean it out and reorganize it to help the colony of bees improve its health and productivity.

I have thought about this issue of whether or not an organization should come to grips with the revitalization of its personnel department when it thinks the department is ailing. In thinking through the matter, I catalogued 21 implications of doing nothing—of walking around the issue and ignoring it. Here they are:

1. *Pyramiding.* A popular tool for administrators who lack

the courage to face up squarely to the task of reorganizing a department is that of "layering," that is, transferring the function and superimposing leadership from another department. Nothing changes in the internal makeup of the target department. It continues to struggle along with its same philosophy, organization, supervision, methods, and devices. However, it is knocked down a notch on the totem pole. For example, in the past the director of personnel may have reported to the deputy chief executive officer. Now he reports to the chief of some staff services group, who in turn reports to the deputy chief executive officer. Pyramiding usually makes a sick department worse, not better. It has a bludgeoning effect on the staff, and it lengthens the lines of communication for those served by the pyramided department.

2. *Reductions in authority.* As the effectiveness of a personnel department dwindles, it runs the risk of having its delegated authorities to consummate personnel actions withdrawn or curtailed. For example, the authority to allocate a new position or to upgrade an existing position can be withdrawn or limited to a certain grade level. The appointment authority can be reduced. The authority to dismiss an employee for cause or to suspend employees without pay can be taken away. Withdrawal of personnel officials from negotiation teams during the labor–management contract renewal season is a serious reduction of authority.

3. *Impact on morale and productivity.* Stagnation and degeneration of morale are natural concomitants of layering. Layering depresses grades, and lowered grades depress salaries and bargaining power of individuals who wish to leave a listing ship. As the abler members of the staff begin their search for outside opportunities, a pall of doubt and insecurity is spread over the work environment. Attendance is affected. The volume and quality of work are noticeably affected.

Obviously, these conditions will be quickly telegraphed to operating groups serviced by the personnel office, and the response level from personnel to operating office requests is likely to be lowered substantially. Rumors will multiply and spread rapidly. Personnel employees with influential outside contacts will pursue these contacts and bring every pressure possible to bear on the situation to protect their tenure. In brief, morale and productivity go from bad to worse.

4. *Reduction in workload.* Operating officials, seeing a stagnating situation in the personnel department, have to review their own options. One of these is to pull back some of the responsibilities they have heretofore been willing to delegate to the personnel department, and proceed on a do-it-yourself basis. For example, they can put forth more effort in recruiting replacements for employees they lose. They can do more training and development on their own initiative if this is a function the personnel office has managed. They can pick up the counseling function and try harder at settling their own grievances. They can do more of the spade work with respect to position classification and wage administration. They can provide the common-need services, communicate more effectively with their employees, keep fuller records and files, and the like.

5. *Budget curtailment.* As workload and the latitude for making ultimate decisions on personnel issues recede, the budget analysts will inevitably sense the opportunity to get their knife into a favorite old enemy. Budget specialists and personnel vie for supremacy in the control of an organization's resources. The result is likely to be a reduction in funding levels for the personnel office when budget people realize that personnel is in trouble with its clients or top management, or both.

Without adequate funds, the personnel department is in deep trouble. It has to let selected positions remain vacant in its staff. It may have to cut back on advertising and rely more on a motley group of hapless walk-in applicants. Hence, any reputation it may have had for presenting quality candidates can decline rapidly. The situation is like an army fighting an expanding war with a diminishing supply of fuel.

6. *Space and facilities contraction.* Next comes the loss of space and a doubling up of staff to make do with less. Furniture that was fitted to larger quarters suddenly looks out of place in cracker-box-type quarters. Some items will not fit at all and have to be surplused. The counselors no longer have private facilities; they have semiprivate facilities. The reception area for job applicants is now improvised, and it no longer has the sparkle and eye appeal it once did. The conference rooms may have been lost altogether, and meetings have to be held in private offices where the distraction from telephones and other noises is counterproductive.

Of all the status symbols, space and the appointments in offices and conference rooms may well be the richest. To the job applicant, the client, and the personnel employee himself, space and facilities are like the uniform and the rank insignia worn by the military person.

7. *Inability to attract new blood of high potential.* As authorities and resources shrink in a personnel department, it becomes increasingly difficult for it to perform one of its mainline functions—to staff the enterprise with high-potential talent. When it cannot commit the employer and has to resort to paperwork to obtain clearances, the insidious delays can cause choice candidates to accept other job offers.

If the department's funds are curtailed, it may well eliminate or drastically reduce its positive recruitment budget, notably, its allocation for advertising vacancies in public media. Another shortcut is to give up background investigations which can make the difference in determining the suitability of a candidate.

8. *Decline of human resources as a profit factor.* The Avis car

rental people seem to have built a fine reputation on the proposition that their employees try harder. However, if the personnel department of Avis were to become a disaster area, and cease to feed into operations quality candidates capable of responding to that challenge, Avis would soon have to change its advertising slogan.

In my own buying habits I have come to favor specialty stores rather than general merchandise stores, because the specialty stores nearly always seem to be staffed with people who know the merchandise better and can be more helpful during a sales transaction. In other words, human resources can be a profit or loss factor. And that is basically why the personnel department exists—to plan, organize, and administer a program to make human resources a profit factor. Nothing can be more serious than circumstances in the personnel department that turn human resources into a loss factor.

9. *Impact on public relations.* Labor unions know where to hit to hurt an employer the most. In the heat of battle to win their objectives in a contract renegotiation, labor leaders will sometimes take a full-page ad in one or more leading metropolitan newspapers.

Our failures in the personnel department to achieve a high level of performance can soon reach the eyes and ears of the general public even without the full-page ad message. A sizable company or public service agency has employees living all over the metropolitan area, and perhaps the state and nation, and they all have friends and social and political contacts. They talk. And to the extent that they bad-mouth the personnel department and the employer generally, public relations are impaired. It can mean a serious loss of image.

10. *More litigation.* There is an increased tendency in these times for people to take their grievances to a court of law. Consumerism is one factor feeding this tendency. There has

been a dramatic increase, for example, in medical malpractice suits. Labor–management relations are also experiencing more litigation.

As the personnel department loses prestige, authority, and resources, inevitably its case load in the courts will increase. Inability to respond to early-warning signs of widening differences between management and labor on specific cases, through investigative and counseling methods, is one source of the mounting litigation. Another factor is the cumulative effect of favorable rulings in the courts from the plaintiffs' standpoint. One favorable ruling may beget a score of new court claims. Hence, the personnel office is again faced with an expanding workload, a diminishing staff, and a residual staff devoid of individuals who had outstanding abilities to deal with labor trouble when its first signs appeared. Experienced personnel are usually the first ones to accept outside offers when they see hard times ahead.

11. *Lowered standing of the enterprise within its industry.* A malfunctioning personnel department soon gets the enterprise in trouble within its industry. The word is passed in trades and crafts and professional circles that the enterprise is having difficulty holding and attracting good people. Suppliers and distributors are alert to a deteriorating situation because it can affect the volume of their own business. It may suggest a cutback in research and development in one company; in another it may mean a shift away from it as the scene of demonstration projects.

Advertising in industrywide media may not feature the particular company whose personnel department is sputtering. High-potential college graduates may stop applying to the organization for first career opportunities. In short, the standing of the organization is diminished within its industry or line of work.

12. *Credit rating impact.* Rating services such as Dun &

Bradstreet are sensitive to deteriorating management effectiveness in enterprises that provide goods and services to the public. Lending agencies rely on these impartial ratings, as well as on their own investigative capabilities, to determine the appropriateness of new loans. Banks monitor their patrons' performance on projects in which bank money is invested. Therefore, when the conditions outlined in this scenario begin to transpire, the credit rating of any marginal organization is in jeopardy. Money may cease to be available except on prohibitive terms. The interest rate may be excessive or the term of the loan may be shortened significantly. The loan applicant may be asked to raise from his own sources a higher percentage of the project cost. In any event, the credit rating serves as a true barometer of management effectiveness as seen by outside financial interests.

13. *Increased union activity; imbalance of power.* As the personnel department ceases to exercise the muscle it had when it was in good standing with top management and when it had ample resources with which to work, labor leaders are likely to increase their pressure for concessions. As in the international political scene, where superpowers of more or less equal strength fall back to coexistence postures, labor and management are less aggressive when they enjoy comparable strength. When the situation is unstable, one side or the other may probe for weakness and step up its demands.

Imbalance is not supportive of organizational health and prosperity, for energies that could be channeled into more productive things suddenly begin to be dissipated in combative activities. Top management will have to use more of its limited time to try to stabilize the situation, and this diversion of attention is always at the expense of policy issues that could be advancing economic interests.

14. *Decisions by fiat.* One of the last stages in any organization suffering from internal difficulties, whether they be in

the personnel department or elsewhere, is that of concentrating the decision-making powers at the very top. Delegations of authority are withdrawn and, even if they aren't, those accustomed to acting on behalf of higher echelons are no longer sure of their ground. They either procrastinate or preclear things before they act.

This abandonment of the participative management style takes its toll among individuals who have traditionally had the will to work and do their best. Decisions come down through channels as cold, formal orders with a minimum of explanation as to why the action is required. Fiats and decrees often beget passive resistance. Those with creativity and innovativeness are discouraged from sharing their ideas on how to produce more goods and services with less effort.

15. *Inability to compete.* The ability to compete in the profit world spells the difference between life and death of an enterprise. We are constantly mindful of this principle in connection with tariffs and international trade. A foreign nation that can make good shoes at lower cost monopolizes the shoe business until the domestic manufacturers improve methods, cut costs, or get the U.S. government to impose or raise the tariff on imported shoes.

An enterprise with a weak personnel department will soon lack the ability to compete, regardless of whether or not it has foreign markets to contend with. The caliber of personnel recruited, morale, labor–management conditions, turnover, and the climate of support from top management are among the factors that affect the ability of an enterprise to compete in its market. It is not likely that any of these will be favorable in an enterprise where the personnel department is malfunctioning.

16. *Infighting by factions.* When an organization is struggling to survive, the various factions that constitute its labor force and management hierarchy begin to undercut each

other and claw at each other's throats. I witnessed such a struggle in a health maintenance organization in early 1978. The staff of physicians had several warring factions, some striking and some on duty. Nurses were separately organized and vying for new benefits. Dentists were on the sidelines, apparently watching with some envy the organized groups compete with one another to see which group could prevail in the contest for leadership and make the greatest gains in bargaining with management.

Each faction had its own legal counsel and sympathizers. The company's services to its membership of over 100,000 persons in a single metropolitan area were severely curtailed. Each side was competing for the attention of the public media. This infighting necessarily subjected the organization to a heavy toll in costs, goodwill, and operating efficiency.

Significantly, during most of this struggle the position of director of personnel was vacant. Representation on the negotiation team for management was provided by the chief executive officer, several members of the board of trustees, and the firm's legal counsel.

17. *Loss of completed-staff-work capability.* The concept of completed staff work is unexcelled as a foundation for sound management. General George C. Marshall, of World War II fame, was a strong advocate of this principle. It is hard enough to gain the full cooperation and understanding of support staffs in the use of the concept when an organization is meeting its service and production goals. When a department such as personnel falls behind in the delivery of services expected of it, the practice of completed staff work becomes exceedingly difficult to sustain. The chief executive officer and his senior staff inevitably will begin to appear at meetings of the corporate board or other policy-making group with a shortfall of completed staff work. The staff is apt to defer to policy makers, that is, to present problems

instead of a series of studied options and a firm recommendation on course of action. The policy group finds itself consumed increasingly by minutiae and the details of how problems developed. It becomes a very frustrating experience for all concerned, and the complexities of the situation are not easily resolved.

18. *System impairment.* When the manpower generator of an organization is functioning improperly, I have found that the organization tends to revert from program-oriented and system-oriented management to crisis management. More and more people in places of responsibility know less and less about their work. They lack the courage to act. They defer to their superiors for decisions instead of acting on their own initiative within the framework of established policy and system.

Essentially, there is a reverse flow of management authority, and the senior officers find themselves presiding over a mounting volume of *case* work in which judgmental decisions are required. Their time to do long-range program planning and development is diminished. Once these habit patterns are formed at subordinate levels, they can harden to the point where top management finds it next to impossible to resystematize the decision-making process.

19. *In-migration of consultants.* When stagnation in an organization becomes fully evident to all concerned, top management may turn to outside consultants to find a cure. This is analogous to the situation within a family when one member falls ill beyond the reach of "home remedies."

If the consultant is worth his salt, he will start by getting all the facts available. This is time-consuming. It can interfere with normal operations. The consulting team has to sift through an avalanche of information, some biased, to discover the true cause-and-effect relationship. This is not easy, regardless of how experienced the consulting team is. And, unfortunately, consultants are not infallible. They can miss in both the diagnostic and prescriptive aspects of their assignment. Their report can, and often does, go dead on the desk of top management. Even if accepted, there can be passive resistance to change from the staff unless management is skilled in the art of institutional change. In other words, the use of consultants is not a sure-fire solution.

20. *Importation of new leadership.* Some directors of personnel have the decency to cast about for another assignment when they sense a loss of confidence in their ability to direct the personnel program. These are the lucky organizations, for it can be hard to fire a weak and ineffective personnel director. It is never a clear-cut case such as proven embezzlement; usually, the case is against a personnel director who is colorless, unimaginative, lacking in self-starting ability, and a confirmed bureaucrat. He may be a product of nepotism or of a promotion-from-within system that did not work very well. Perhaps he is a disabled veteran for whom the employer felt some obligation or compassion. How does one deal decisively, expeditiously, and compassionately with such a case? My answer can be found in Part II of this book.

New leadership may or may not restore personnel administration to a healthy and useful state. At best, it will take time. The new leadership may have to rebuild the philosophy, policies, and procedures of the personnel department. It may have to install a new senior staff. It will doubtless have to rebuild relationships with operating officials and institute a program of mainline functions and services, as outlined in Chapter 4. There can never be any compromise in the choice of the best qualified leadership available for the personnel department. No other key will fit.

21. *Injury to personnel administration as a profession.* When a private or public enterprise fails for lack of sound personnel administration, the art of personnel administration as a de-

serving profession suffers a stunning blow. Enough blows to the head will eventually kill any viable entity. Our profession has won very few blue ribbons for brilliance. It needs successes, not failures, to build its national standing as a worthy contributor to the art of management. Certainly the overwhelming bipartisan support that the Congress of the United States gave President Carter's drastic civil service reform measure in 1978 was no tribute to the way personnel administration was functioning after nearly a century of experience with the merit system in national government.

It is my own feeling that personnel administration has measured up well against the strictest standards only in widely scattered public and private organizations. The professional societies that serve our profession need more forward-looking members who are able and willing to articulate new methods and follow through with prototype building, testing, and reporting. Too much professional-society activity in personnel administration is a regurgitation of old ideas, some of which have in my judgment never worked.

Part II

A Three-Stage Program for Recovery

Chapter 4

Stage One: Revamping the Personnel Department

THE PRECEDING CHAPTERS have stressed my judgment that the performance of our personnel departments generally leaves much to be desired. There is an urgent need for reform, not only in the private but also in the public sector. Notwithstanding the broad sweep of the 1978 federal civil service reform package, I believe many problems will remain, especially in the departments and the agencies. There will also remain thousands of state and municipal personnel systems in need of review.

This and the following two chapters offer a three-stage approach to reform: (1) revamping the personnel department, (2) improving the scope and the quality of personnel service (discussed in Chapter 5), and (3) providing for continuing growth and development of the personnel staff (the subject matter of Chapter 6). Chapter 7 is a blueprint for getting started with the personnel system reform; in addition, it suggests some milestones to watch for after the personnel system is revamped.

Revamping is not a job the personnel department can do for itself. Top management must take an active role in reshaping the mission, organization, leadership, and philosophy of the personnel department. This revamping process involves at least four major steps:

1. Realigning the personnel department's mission and functions.
2. Reforming the selection of personnel department leadership.
3. Reforming the personnel department's presence.
4. Increasing the personnel department's responsiveness.

STEP 1: REALIGNING THE PERSONNEL DEPARTMENT'S MISSION AND FUNCTIONS

Realignment can be accomplished by (1) clearly defining the personnel department's role, (2) identifying and strengthening its mainline functions, (3) freeing the personnel department from misplaced functions, and (4) distributing personnel administration authorities and responsibilities appropriately between the central department and local branches.

Defining the Personnel Department's Role

Many personnel departments honestly do not understand their role. Some staffs seem to relate more to law enforcement than they do to sound personnel administration and industrial relations. They are ready to throw their book of regulations at any operating official for an infraction. Some members of the staff see themselves in such roles as social workers, ombudsmen, paperwork mechanics, investigators, interviewers, campaign solicitors, bill collectors, and assorted other practitioners. They have great difficulty in distinguishing between the "meat" of their mission and the peripheral things that have come to rest in the personnel department like tumbleweeds.

The chain-of-command question is the first role question in need of an answer. I see the personnel director as I see all other employees—an individual who deserves to know who his boss is, and someone who must never have more than one boss. Top management should, of course, identify the senior executive to whom the personnel director is to report, and this should be done in writing by official notice and preferably accompanied by an organization chart to show relationships. Hopefully, the personnel director's relationship will be directly with the general manager or executive vice president of a private company or with the senior political administrator of a public service agency. Any notions the personnel director may have about being an ombudsman for employees is pure fantasy.

A dressier title for the personnel director in the private sector, and the one I like, is executive vice president for personnel administration and industrial relations. Note the emphasis on industrial relations in the title. The personnel director is no longer conducting a friendly game of "employee relations" between employees and management or among various groups of employees themselves. His organization is locked into a hardened set of relationships between management and labor organizations. The periodical formal dialog is through negotiation, bargaining, mediation, binding arbitration, or strikes.

Industrial relations may work as a separate entity in some organizations. Where it does, there may well be a good reason; in any event, it is worth examining the need for such a separation closely. Circumstances may have changed to the point where the two interrelated facets of personnel administration can be welded back together and placed under unified leadership. If now is not the right time, top management should keep on its agenda the possibility of combining and rearranging the two functions.

The personnel department has four target audiences of prime importance. The overriding principle guiding all personnel departments is that they exist to render *service* to others. They do not exist primarily to *control* or *regulate* the lives and work of employees. We should be discouraged at every turn when we begin to see our role as one of operating an intricate system of "gates and locks." The prime target audiences (clients) to be served by the personnel department are:

Top management.
Line and staff supervisors and managers.
Employees generally.
Job applicants.

Serving Top Management

Top management needs a great deal of continuing wise advice and counsel on human resources issues. The following areas of concern are illustrative of the ways in which the personnel department can support top management.

Organizational refinements. The modern business enterprise is dynamic. It responds to changes in technology, markets, labor conditions, the trends of the economy, and many other factors. The personnel department can facilitate the necessary organizational and leadership changes to accommodate dynamism.

Organizations often succeed or fail on the basis of how well they fit their organizational patterns to people. The personnel department presumably has insights into the people who are eligible for consideration for leadership roles. If its records management and other personnel systems are functioning well, it has a balanced picture of the total past performance and potential of employees.

Filling executive leadership positions. Filling an executive leadership position when the choice is not obvious and easy is very hard work. It is also time-consuming when it is done well. Top management needs good staff support on this task. Before applications are entertained, the personnel department may want to counsel top management on some restructuring of the vacant position. Perhaps the last three incumbents have failed on the job because of an impossible combination of duties and responsibilities. The compensation and fringe benefits for the position may be out of line with the market or with comparable in-house positions. The qualification standards for the position may also need updating due to social and economic factors.

Pressures can mount for filling a vacancy immediately. The person with seniority may expect to move up, but his marginal qualifications and a dearth of in-house talent suggest a look outside. This can require a massive effort—active recruitment, communications, vouching of references, search panel activity, and special screening through assessment centers, retreats, group oral interviews, and other procedures. The personnel department should be the focal point for the search and selection operations.

Labor–management relations. Unionization of an organization may have occurred in the first place because its personnel administration policies and practices were ineffective and negative in tone. Employees could no longer deal individually and get satisfactory results, so they banded together in a union or employee association. Management can err a second time by staffing the labor relations office of its personnel department with negative, inept, and provocative individuals. This staff must be keen, imaginative, well informed, industrious, articulate, and responsive. Its full-time job is to cultivate and maintain a favorable state of labor–management relations. Top management should listen when it has something to say.

The labor relations staff should embody a variety of skills, including legal, medical, engineering, economic, and managerial. It also needs a reservoir of rich, practical experience from encounters with labor groups. The labor relations staff will have a certain amount of good faith credit with labor if it has been fair and just in adjudicating claims and grievances. The issues on which this staff can counsel and negotiate run the whole gamut of personnel administration.

Incentives. Motivation is a mysterious factor that is generally accepted as a stimulant to the will to work. Our personnel departments have traditionally given more lip service to the concept than they have given practical effort. We can recite the findings of important behavioral science studies, starting with the Hawthorne Plant studies led by Roethlisberger in the 1930s; but that is about as far as our interest and involvement in incentives seem to go.

I recently participated in a selection panel in which medical doctors with administrative experience were being considered for the chief executive officer position of a major health care organization. I put to one of the candidates the question, "What do you consider the most fulfilling work experience of your whole 20-year career, and why?" He described a work scene in an organization where morale and productivity were low. He was new to the organization and unfamiliar with causal factors. He discovered that there were no incentives in use but that there were some to which employees would certainly respond if they were instituted.

Combining a system of realistic incentives for team performance with a system of quality control, he was able to turn the operation completely around. Top management found the results so profitable that it institutionalized his plan successively on divisional, regional, national, and international scales. This institutionalization was apparently a source of tremendous pride and feeling of self-fulfillment by the doctor. He described it with a radiant gleam in his eyes.

It is my belief that the American work scene is ripe for the use of practical incentives tied to a system of group performance and quality controls. One has to remember that Maslow's hierarchy of human needs does not put pay at the top of the pyramid. Just as it was not in the case of the doctor just mentioned, it is not in the case of the typical John or Mary who work outside their homes. We cannot discover what the incentives need to be from our swivel chairs. We have to rout around in the humdrum tasks of people who turn out the products and services of the organization. That accounts for the emphasis on organization and job analysis in the model personnel department suggested later in this chapter.

A personnel department does not easily come by the insights needed for advising top management and operating officials on incentives without knowing every operation and every job, and how jobs interrelate. Painstaking, on-the-scene observation and analysis are required. What if the U.S. Department of Agriculture had tried to run its Extension Service without county agents, or with county agents who had a well-appointed office and, though always "on duty," never traveled and visited farmers on their farms and farmers' wives in their kitchens? I have always been impressed with how the Extension Service uses the principle of incentives to stimulate better agricultural and home economics practices among farm families; the price, clearly, is extensive field work.

Budget formulation and execution. There are many opportunities for the personnel department to make a more constructive input into the budget formulation and execution than it traditionally has. Personnel people and budget people tend to be natural enemies vying for control of the lifeblood of their parent organization—its money and its human resources—almost like the fable of the sun and the wind vying for supremacy and testing their comparative strength by seeing which force could cause the pedestrian to remove his jacket.

The budget is a superior instrument of planning. It is a mistake to reason that dollar-minded specialists (the budget group) should have an "exclusive" over this instrument of planning, and that people-minded specialists (the personnel group) should stay in the background and take no active part until the budget has been debated, perhaps meat-axed, and finally appropriated and allocated.

The personnel department has far more occasion to maintain a day-to-day dialog with line and staff groups than the budget office does. Its interest in organization and job analysis, staffing, compensation, and employee relations is ever-widening and ever-deepening. It knows the state of labor–management relations, the labor market, turnover trends, retirement schedules, and relationships among incentives, motivation, and performance. It can project economic demands from unions and the timetable for manpower solutions to current and foreseeable problems.

For example, the time it takes to recruit and develop young managers or young professionals of any kind is a known quantity. This in turn may affect the rate of decentralization, expansion of output, marketing, need for capitalization, public relations, and many other budget planning factors. The personnel department has too frequently been a silent partner in the budget processes except when presenting its own requirements.

Employment policy. Next we need to visualize the personnel department's role in employment policy as it affects its parent organization's thinking at the top. Some personnel departments work like the bell captain in a hotel. They wait for their bell to jingle or for someone to walk up with a complaint or request. Advice and counsel to top management on employment policy has a backdrop of intricately woven fabric—mission, tradition, civil rights legislation, labor–management agreements, prevailing practice among other employers competing in the labor market for skills, long-range goals of the organization, and the like. The personnel director alone can't and shouldn't make the decisions on employment policy. He would be taking the fate of his parent organization and its departments in his hands, concentrating rather than spreading the risks. It is an area in which true leadership and corporate citizenship are needed.

For example, an employment policy to move more women into executive leadership roles takes courage in the face of opposing tradition. So do the policy of passing over people with seniority when the qualifications of younger people clearly surpass the seniors, the decision to reach outside for superior talent in preference to using the promotion-from-within policy, and the decision to contract out a function when a contractor can do the work more economically and efficiently than in-house personnel.

Procurement policy. Our personnel departments need to be active in policy formulation with respect to procurement. The procurement people, like the budget people, can become an autonomous kingdom. The goods and services procured by any organization are for the use of its human resources. In personnel, we should be making studies on motivation and productivity. Personnel recruits people, cooperates in their training and development, records their performance, hears their complaints, and separates them from the payroll for various reasons. It understands their health and safety problems. It is a natural source of contributions to procurement policy. It may well be possible to enhance the real incentives system through procurement policy without serious effects on procurement costs.

Serving Line and Staff Supervisors and Managers

The operating personnel office should provide a full range of support services to supervisors and managers of line and staff groups. Emphasis will normally be on staffing, position classification, promotions and transfers, pay and fringe benefits administration, and counseling.

As the "backbone" of management, supervisors and managers deserve maximum personnel support. To the extent that the personnel office impedes work of the operator, it shares the responsibility for mission failures.

Supervisors and managers need as much counseling as any other group of employees, and sometimes more. A new supervisor may feel insecure. Perhaps he or she has inherited a group of employees about whom very little is known except what the outgoing supervisor mentioned hurriedly. Some subordinates may have an involved case history in the personnel office. The subordinates may also have had complaints of their own. All of this background needs to be evaluated and considered before the new supervisor takes any new initiatives.

A manager may feel that his operation has changed substantially since it was last examined by the position classification unit for pay purposes. He may want to try some job enrichment in order to challenge several employees to new performance levels. The manager needs help from the personnel office in these matters.

Wherever people are working, there is a need for "people mechanics," for people are far more complex than computers. What if the computer industry were not backstopped by an on-call corps of computer technicians? Interestingly, these technicians are kept abreast of their trade partly by computers. Computer-assisted instruction (CAI), remotely based, is used to explain (on local output units) solutions to difficult problems in troubleshooting and repair of computers. There is no "CAI" to attend to the *personnel needs* of the human beings who have to operate and repair computers, nor for others. The technical assistance is available—or should be—in the operating personnel office. Unfortunately, new employees are not accompanied by anything comparable to an "owner's operating manual."

Serving Employees Generally

The operating personnel office should be like a department store—a one-stop place where the shopper can satisfy nearly any household need he has. However, it is not easy to attract employees to a personnel office with a bad image, especially one that represents the voice of *management.* The personnel office is not an ombudsman. It is there to protect the interests of management in every way possible. Why, therefore, would an employee ever be inclined to go near a personnel office?

Management has reasoned that there are economic advantages to be gained by doing some things for employees. To the employee, the services the personnel office offers on behalf of management can be like the "free samples" of products we all receive in the mail from time to time. To reject these "free services" of the personnel office would be foolish, and the personnel office would be foolish to administer them sluggishly, ineptly, or inequitably. It is the best opportunity we have for demonstrating that management is genuinely concerned.

Here, the lesson learned in the Hawthorne plant experiment is relevant: When employees see management as being genuinely concerned about their welfare, they will strive to produce more. Management could profit by applying this lesson more intelligently in rendering personnel services for employees.

The range of services to be rendered is limited only by the imagination and budget of the personnel staff. The clearinghouse role is central to such services. Someone wants to get into a car pool. Someone needs help on housing. Another wants to get into a hobby group. People like to buy and sell things informally. Travel charters interest some. Loans, savings, investments, welfare assistance, and other financial matters vitally concern others. An employee may want some vocational counseling, or someone to listen to a grievance. He may need a Notary Public. He occasionally wants access to his employment history or help in satisfying credit-bureau and lending-agency inquiries. Emergency room services are necessary at times for a minor illness or accident.

These are only illustrative of the many services a truly supportive personnel office can provide the employee. Employees will solve their problems one way or another, with or without the personnel office's help. When they lose confidence in the personnel office, it will cost the employer double. First, employees will begin going outside for help, taking more and more time off from work, and the time off will often not get charged to their leave accounts. Secondly, the employees will conclude, after a few trips outside, and perhaps some harassment from their supervisors, that they are stuck with a thoughtless or miserly employer. This can quickly start an erosion of the personnel office image, a decline of incentive, and economic losses.

Serving Job Applicants

The future of any enterprise depends on its ability to attract and hold replacements and persons to fill new positions required by the growth of the enterprise. The personnel office should have a vital role in planning and managing this flow of manpower. Job applicants may gain lasting impressions from the experience they have during the first encounter at the personnel office. Inefficiency, indifference, rudeness, impersonal treatment, prejudice, and ignorance are inexcusable in personnel offices, but I continue to see them on full display there.

I am reserving the last chapter of this book for a detailed discussion of this clientele of the personnel office. Job applicants are frequently walking around the personnel department and trying to get the attention of people in whom they have more confidence. It is time we try to reestablish ourselves as the front door.

Strengthening the Personnel Department's Mainline Functions

Mainline functions of the personnel department need identification and strengthening. We do not always put first things first in the personnel department. If we were given only two functions to manage, they would probably be the employment of people and the administration of compensation systems. Everything else we do should therefore be supportive of these mainline functions. For example, organization and job analysis surveys tell the department more about organizational relationships and specific job requirements. This information in turn can improve recruitment, selection, and placement. It can also help us advise and counsel line and staff executives, managers, and supervisors on how to better utilize their human resources for maximum productivity and service.

Personnel departments attract nonessential activities, and it is not uncommon for one of these activities to be staffed and to work its way into the formal organizational fabric. For example, payroll operations are closely related to personnel operations because they depend on the notification of official personnel action as a source document. To let payroll become entrenched in the personnel department is a serious mistake. It absorbs staff time like a sponge, for it always has to move with clock-like precision. General adjustments in pay can generate numerous questions, overtime work, and stressful conditions that rob the personnel staff of time it needs for dealing with vital policy issues.

Besides the peripheral functions that drift into the personnel department, there is the tendency to produce its own manpower supply. A personnel clerk is a personnel clerk today and, too often, an "employment officer" or a "classification analyst" tomorrow. Promotion-from-within policies have a great deal of merit—provided the standards are not compromised by the makers of the standards in taking care of their own.

Any trade is "apprenticeable" perhaps, but the work of the personnel specialist cannot be learned in a day or a week. I have known many cases of personnel departments using a double standard—one for its client departments and one for its own department. It is extremely difficult to write a standard that leaves no discretion to the employment officer. Any good standard allows the substitution of experience for formal education. Merit concepts can be compromised in the evaluation of the substitutable experience, choice of evaluator, appeal of in-shop candidate, and the special considerations that always crop up.

This is one of the weakest links in the whole personnel system in many organizations. It is essentially the issue of who is to protect the protectors of the merit system against themselves. To the extent that we are human and succumb to our emotions instead of our best judgment in applying the standards, the personnel department can eventually be marred with mediocrity. Many personnel departments promote from within when they should reach outside for superior talent. They prematurely advance individuals from the clerical ranks to a professional position without requiring them to subject themselves to an intensive course of study to gain the necessary knowledge, skills, ability, and philosophical insights to cope with the demands of the work. It places individuals in decision-making positions who have not been seasoned through an understudy role.

This whole process of diluting the strength of the mainline personnel functions can take its toll from the operating departments and other staff groups of the organization. When the personnel specialist lacks the proper value system or intellectual framework for contributing positively to ongoing operations, the organization is in deep trouble. In other words, as goes the health of the personnel department, so goes the health of the parent organization. Management either has to isolate the personnel department and relegate it to "leaf-raking" chores or subject it to a thorough top-to-bottom revitalization. This is seldom done. Personnel departments, like bramble bush undergrowth, are not easily penetrated. People tend to walk around them in order to get to where they want to go.

Freeing the Personnel Department from Inappropriate Functions

There are many commonly neglected functions of personnel departments that are in fact inappropriate and should be transferred to other departments. The personnel department has followed a policy of "colonialism" with respect to certain management functions that initially sounded compatible with its own mission. These colonized functions have been tucked away in its empire—and neglected. Neglected in ways not unlike the ways in which the nations of the colonialized world were neglected before their dawn of independence. They have been left woefully underdeveloped, exploited, and hurting from frustration.

Five examples of such neglected functions that many personnel departments, both private and public, have colonized but neglected are employee training and development, safety, manpower planning, performance standards, and hours of duty. Let me say a few things about each of these within the context of my own experience. Remember that these examples are not a complete inventory of neglected functions, but they are illustrative and may help you find others in your own personnel department.

Employee training and development. Recently, I met the chief of employee training and development for an organization operating nationally with over 10,000 employees. I asked him if he feels adequately staffed for the responsibility he is carrying. He readily confided that he is not; then he mentioned a long list of nontraining and nondevelopment functions that have been switched into his bailiwick. Here they are: suitability, security, awards, retirement, discipline cases, life insurance, health insurance, and alcohol and drug abuse. And doubtless there are others he could mention in a quiet moment when he is not being harassed by this collection of responsibilities that belong elsewhere.

Personnel departments are notorious for assigning unrelated functions to the training and development office. The personnel director is under heavy pressure to deliver on what he knows are his mainline functions—to fill vacancies, classify jobs, run the pay system, and keep a hand in labor–management relations. He sees no presence of the staff development people in these operations. They never bail him out of a crisis with top management or operations people. He sees the training and development role as being an auxiliary, low-burner-type function. Therefore, he sees nothing wrong with saddling the staff development office with work he cannot assign to his mainline groups without jeopardizing their capacity to respond rapidly to operating demands.

Safety. Industrial safety is as important to industrial organizations as their assembly lines. The health, safety, productive capacity, and morale of their work force depend upon it. The responsibility for all aspects of industrial safety, including safety education and training, therefore belongs to line managers and not to the personnel department.

There are many facets to safety. These include such factors as plant and office layout, equipment design, employee wearing apparel, noise, color dynamics, sequencing of operations, attitudes, quality control, supervision, maintenance practices, fatigue, and countless others. To determine the cause of an accident, one may need the finest detective because of the many variables.

Several disciplines are needed to combat safety hazards. The first requirement is an imaginative and highly skilled engineer. Some engineers have interdisciplinary training and are rated as safety engineers. They presumably have some knowledge of the major engineering subdisciplines including architectural, industrial, mechanical, electrical, and chemical. The safety engineer should be able at least to diagnose the engineering problem and to know where to get any highly specialized help he needs. This engineer does not belong in the personnel department, since he has little or nothing in common with personnel specialists.

Next to engineering, probably the most important discipline is education and training. Seemingly, this aspect of the safety program should be grouped with other employee training and development activities. I disagree, for to split the education and training role of safety away from the safety engineer is to place it in a two-boss position.

The size of the parent organization is critical here. A giant organization will have a sizable safety group. A small concern will perhaps not be able to afford more than one employee on safety. If that person is an engineer, he or she should also handle the education and training assignments; it makes no sense to split them. If there are several engineers and the personnel department is sufficiently interested and active in safety from an industrial relations standpoint, the thing to do may be to have the safety office detach one of its safety engineers on indefinite detail and station him in the personnel department. He can then maintain a continuous dialog with the labor relations experts and the medical and legal specialists who are dealing on a day-to-day basis with operational problems.

Some organizations try to economize on safety by making it everybody's business. Consequently, it becomes the responsibility of no one, and accountability is lost. The personnel department has little or no business in safety. Operating officials are ill-advised to give up control of this vital function.

Manpower planning. I believe this is another area in which the personnel department should just not venture. Subject matter specialists in the operating departments who do the conceptual planning for the development and distribution of new products and services are the ones in the best position to make manpower projections. Planning is a recognized profession in the United States. The personnel department has no professionally qualified planners.

Manpower planning is an intricate process requiring a knowledge of factors which only the subject matter specialists in line and certain staff groups have access to and fully comprehend. Production goals and objectives, marketing schedules, and impending changes from technology, government regulations and guidelines, and consumerism are some examples of the pertinent factors. To reason that anyone can plan is a mistake. The personnel department can contribute some information to the manpower planning process, but it should not have the primary planning responsibility. Even a professionally trained planner, if positioned in the personnel department, would be separated from the vital data and other indicators he needs.

Performance standards. Our personnel departments have talked about this concept for years, but without much to show in practical results. Performance standards cannot be "legislated." We lack the knowledge of production capabilities and technology to set precise standards. Standards are one of the crunch issues in labor–management negotiation at contract renewal time. If the personnel department is to play a central role in such negotiations, it must rely on some good staff work done in advance. The on-the-scene staff with continuity of experience is in operations, not personnel.

Participative management approaches to the proper development of performance standards would require a dialog between employees affected and their production managers and supervisors, not with us in the personnel office. We are regarded as outsiders and our motives are often suspect. While we have no license for coordinating the development of performance standards, we should be strong advocates, facilitators, and recorders of such efforts. Developing performance standards requires a sound grasp of operations, technology, production methods, working conditions, the experience level and caliber of each individual in the work force, and other relevant data. It is the product of careful analysis of performance data combined with a give-and-take dialog of responsible people from labor and line management.

Setting Hours of Duty. The personnel department is bluffing when it purports to be the one that sets hours of duty in an organization. Setting hours of duty is a function of production and service people. The peculiarities of incoming and outgoing work (for instance, work controlled by commercial transportation schedules) are controlling factors. The personnel department can be one of the negotiators on issues affecting the basic work week, holidays, overtime pay, excused absences, and the administration of leave.

We should be contributing in this area by promoting more imaginative uses of part-time workers, such as spouses available for part-time work outside the home, students, teachers, the elderly, handicapped persons, and the underemployed. Our record in the use of part-time workers has been mighty poor.

Distributing Personnel Authority and Responsibilities

The personnel director needs to exercise certain authorities and responsibilities in the central personnel department and to delegate other responsibilities to local personnel units and to the line officials and other staff officials. The ultimate responsibility for the quality of personnel administration and industrial relations is nontransferable. The central department is accountable to the chief executive officer of the company or public service agency.

In my view, the objectives of personnel administration are better served when there is a liberal decentralization of authority to act on personnel matters. It is a central theme of this book that operating officials lose control of the destiny of their production and service programs when they are deprived of authority to act directly on personnel matters. The manager who cannot hire, fire, promote, reassign, or transfer an employee without prior approval of the personnel department is in dire straits.

Role of the Central Personnel Department

There are four major types of authority that should be exercised centrally by the personnel department. They are:

1. The establishment of personnel administration goals and objectives.
2. The formulation of personnel administration policies, programs, systems, procedures, standards, and guidelines.
3. To function as an intermediary, catalyst, documentor, and reporter.
4. To be a fact-finder, adviser, consultant, and teacher.

The organization chart in Figure 1 depicts my version of a model central personnel department and its specific responsibilities, with the executive vice president for personnel administration and industrial relations (director of personnel in the public sector) providing overall leadership in personnel administration and industrial relations.

Several of the functions depicted in Figure 1 may not be self-explanatory to the reader. You will note that the associate director for planning, development, and results has the responsibility for completing the "loop" in his work. He plans, develops, tests, and critically examines for results. I have borrowed a concept from practicing journalists—investigative reporting—to help him find out what results actually are obtained from programs he conceptualizes and releases to local personnel units and operating personnel. He

Figure 1. Model Personnel Department

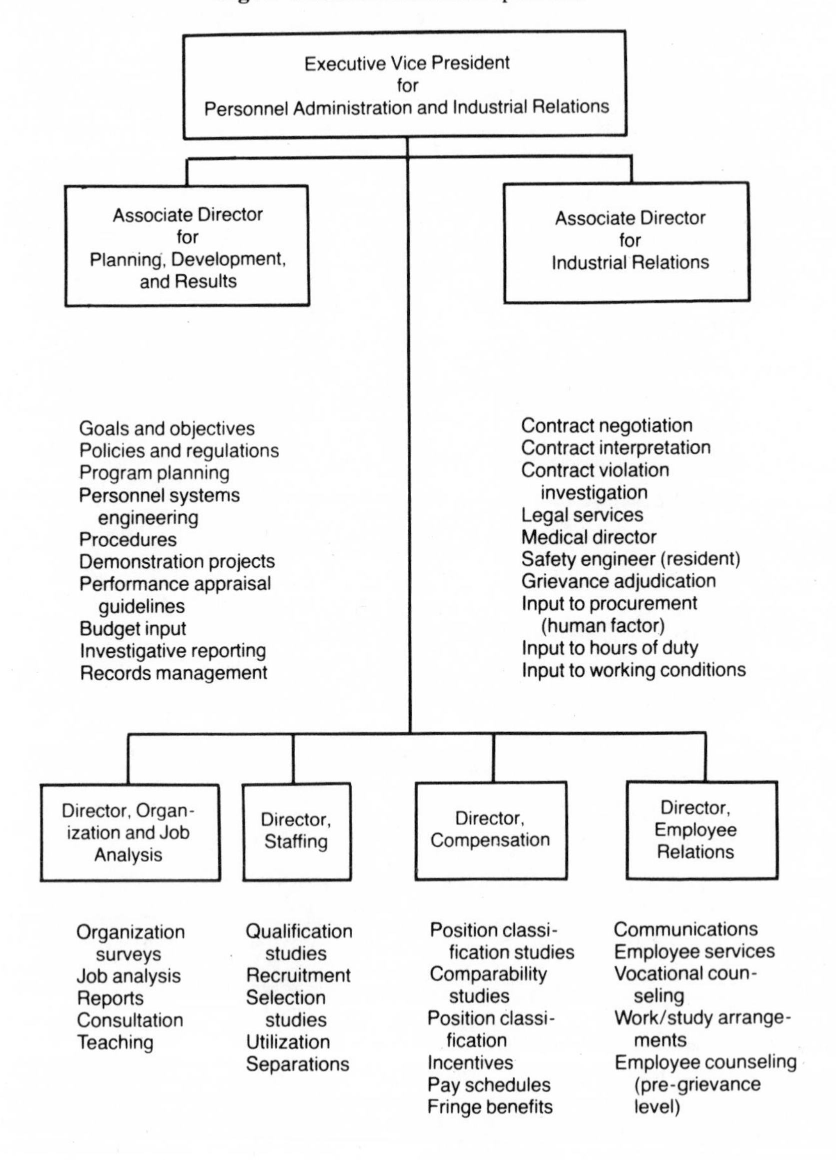

has a vested interest in seeing to it that the applicant and the employee have been dealt with judiciously, expeditiously, and compassionately.

Organizations have all sorts of control mechanisms to safeguard against embezzlement and other forms of fraud where money, materials, and equipment are at stake. They have controllers, inspectors general, quality control experts, store detectives, security guards, videotape cameras, and other safeguards. But what does *management* offer to assure that the employee gets a fair deal from his department or from us in the personnel office? For this assurance, I believe, the typical employee has decided he has to look to organized labor.

Budget input. A second thought that deserves special mention in relation to the associate director for planning, development, and results is that of budget input. The budget is a superb instrument of planning for any organization. Too frequently the personnel department and the budget department are found walled off from one another on separate islands that are as unapproachable as a fortress surrounded by a moat.

It is my strong belief that the personnel department should be a major influence in budget formulation. Its senior staff should not be observers at budget hearings; they should be active participants on panels of expert budget examiners. My model assigns organization and job analysis as one of four mainline operating functions of the personnel department. Through data continuously being assembled by organization and job analysis, the personnel department could be one the best informed panelists in budget hearings. It should be active in the allotment of funds, in curtailments and accelerations of spending, and in long-range fiscal policy determination.

Procurement input. Procurement people, like budget people

(and personnel people), can be carried away with their importance and become indifferent to opportunities for collaboration with other knowledgeable and interested members of the management family. This is the case, I believe, with respect to the procurement of things and services by the procurement department.

Procurement aims to provide the land, space, equipment, materials, systems, and services needed by the *people* of the organization. The personnel office has a vital interest in these same people. It finds them, formally employs them, attends to many of their individual needs, hears their grievances, and monitors their productivity, health, and welfare. Why shouldn't it be interested in the design of their chairs and work benches, vehicles, tools, and work environment? I believe it has a valid interest in procurement and that it should regularly make a "human factor" input to procurement policy and to the actual procurement of common-use items.

Organization surveys and job analysis. Organization surveys and job analysis also deserve special mention. We all know that informal organization is as universal as formal organization, but I am afraid those of us in the personnel department are inclined to forget it. Unless we make regular organization surveys, we soon lose awareness of the fact that operating officials go right on adapting their organizational relationships to program changes and to the human resources and technology they have to work with. The personnel department, in turn, continues to use outdated qualification standards, performance appraisal guidelines, position classification standards, and pay schedules.

Organization surveys and job analysis are interdependent, since organizational adjustments often change job requirements and vice versa. We in personnel should stop giving only lip service to our organization survey and job analysis responsibilities. They are mainline functions.

Role of the Operating Personnel Office

The central personnel department should be the model or prototype builder and tester. This leaves the operating personnel office the role of emulating the model and, in accordance with the policies and standards set by the central personnel department, achieving common goals and objectives in a unified program of personnel administration. The local unit is also responsible for developing a body of recorded experience to enable the central personnel department to continue and further refine its planning, development, and assessment of results.

The chart in Figure 1 should be read in this light. Table 1 lists several examples that illustrate the relationship between the two levels of personnel administration.

Table 1. Comparison of the roles of the central personnel department and local personnel units for selected functions.

Function	*Role of Central Personnel Department*	*Role of Local Personnel Units*
Organization surveys and job analysis	Build survey models.	Make surveys and share data with local clients; provide information copies to central unit for analysis, publication, and further distribution.
Qualification standards	Develop and publish qualification standards.	Perform recruitment and selection activities, guided by qualification standards. Make input to establishment of new and updating of old standards.
Position classification standards	Develop position classification standards.	Apply standards in classifying positions. Make input to developing new and updating old standards.

Role of Line and Staff Managers in Personnel Administration

There is whole array of personnel responsibilities that should reside primarily in the hands of line and staff officials, with local personnel units being *supportive* and handling any personnel functions which the line and staff groups prefer not to attempt themselves. Here is an illustrative list of a dozen personnel functions that should be delegated to line and staff groups:

Manpower planning.
Establishment of performance standards.
Performance appraisals and counseling.
Inputs to labor–management contracts.
Safety engineering and safety education and training.
Setting hours of duty.
Establishing working conditions.
Advising on organizational relationships.
Recruitment.
Selection.
Promotions, transfers, reassignments, and details (temporary job reassignments).
Administration of incentives.

To delegate primary authority and responsibility for these personnel functions is not to say that the local personnel unit is completely relieved of its authority and responsibility. It should back the operating people at every turn, making them look good by pointing the way and guiding them—but always with a passion for anonymity. It has a post-audit role to ensure that policies and standards have been observed. It has a teaching (show-how) role in the early stages of a new personnel administration experience for an operating manager or supervisor. It has a catalytic role to get a multiplier effect for practical solutions to common problems. With this reversal of roles between the operating offical and the personnel specialist, I believe we personnel specialists can soon win a place on the production and service teams of any organization and greatly improve the image of our end of the business.

STEP 2: REFORMING THE SELECTION OF PERSONNEL DEPARTMENT LEADERSHIP

No national sport could long survive if its main source of players and coaches were water boys, locker room attendants, scoreboard clerks, and camp followers. I am almost convinced that the underlying cause of our personnel departments' troubles is the incestuous practice of trying to produce "professionals" from people whose basic qualifications are insufficient. I know of a survey made by a national organization to determine who was most likely to emerge as the personnel officer in its field establishments. The data pointed to former secretaries of personnel directors.

Qualifications Needed

Former secretaries to personnel directors may be as good a source of candidates as any other, provided the work at the secretarial level is sufficiently motivating to encourage the candidate to engage in a well-ordered program of in-house and outside education and training to develop his or her professional capabilities.

It is my considered judgment that six basic competencies are needed by the "first team" (senior staff) in an effective personnel department. I include the personnel director, the two associate directors of personnel, and the heads of the four mainline functions shown in the chart of a model personnel department (see Figure 1). Each of the competencies is described below.

1. *Substantive background*. If I should ever become the majority stockholder in a large pharmaceutical company, I would feel safer about my investment if the personnel director were a competent chemist. The same goes for other businesses. Thus I would prefer an engineer as personnel director of a construction firm, an economist as personnel director of a banking network, a journalist as personnel director of a publishing house, a medical doctor as personnel director of a health maintenance organization.

You can reason that this is a waste of talent, that the ultimate decisions in personnel administration can be decentralized and delegated by a personnel director without technical background to subject matter specialists who manage ongoing operations. You may also reason that a subject matter specialist in the personnel administration facet of management or any other facet will soon revert to his chemist or journalist role and neglect his managerial reponsiblities.

I say it is not so if you choose well among the available candidates. To step at least temporarily out of one's narrow and ever-deepening groove of specialization to the higher ground of a personnel director's role and to contribute to the long-range manpower capabilities of an organization can be one of the most fulfilling experiences of one's whole life-long career. And think of the additional insights subject matter specialists bring to the task. They can draw from experiences gained at every turn up the "spiral staircase" of professional growth as they assess the need for human resources and act to meet the needs. They can guide their staff to better recruitment sources, oversee better job design, devise better systems of incentives and compensation, identify personnel people who can better influence labor–management relations, and contribute ideas for improving organization.

2. *Technical skills*. The technical skills required in personnel administration and industrial relations at the policy level

can be learned relatively quickly if one has a subject matter base on which to weld them. There will always be a dearth of candidates for the personnel department senior staff positions who are "double majors" in a relevant subject matter field and personnel administration. My proposition is this: if you have to settle for one or the other, give preferential consideration to individuals who are subject matter specialists and who have an adequate proficiency in the five other skill areas identified below.

Personnel administration at the policy level is a matter of formulating and administering equitably and efficiently a body of goals and objectives, policies, standards, guidelines, systems, and methods in order to provide for the continuity of production and service operations in the parent organization. To do this well, one needs a clear understanding of the organization's history and mission, a philosophy, unwavering commitment, and a successful experience at progressively responsible levels in using the six competencies herein called for. There is no magic to personnel administration. For individuals from such disciplines as chemistry, journalism, engineering, and economics, the logic and tools they are accustomed to using need not be laid aside. Obviously, a thorough indoctrination and familiarization with new reference materials is needed by the subject matter specialist. Intensive learning can come from seminars and workshops conducted by professional societies and educational institutions.

3. *Human skills*. Candidates for employment often tell the interviewer, "I like to work with people." Of course, some individuals are not as effective as they perceive themselves to be in human relations. Their attitudes may have hardened in childhood or during some work experience, and these attitudes may be incompatible with modern thinking. For example, some men still cannot visualize women in certain lines of work. Are we human beings in personnel offices

completely free of attitudes and biases that could hamper us?

The members of the personnel department's senior staff need the interaction and team support they can get from each other. Integrated personnel administration is the best kind. It takes individuals who are skilled in interpersonal relations and whose sensitivities are highly developed to make the senior staff a cohesive and smoothly functioning team. When one program ignores another and engages in unilateral action, the whole mission suffers. Senior staff members need to know each other as individuals, their strengths and limitations, and their special interests and backgrounds. They must be people-oriented and radiate a sense of pride in the organization and its mission, belief in its human resources, compassion, and enthusiasm for the broad mission.

These human skills can be acquired, but not overnight. It is better that the senior staff in the personnel department bring them to the assignment and not try to do more than hone them sharper as they work there. Much of our image problem, I believe, comes from our own human skill shortages. The senior personnel official sets the tone for subordinates. If he or she is a contrary, uncompromising, legalistic person, with transparent suspicion of employees generally and operating supervisors and managers in particular, junior professionals and even the receptionist and file clerk may soon behave similarly.

4. *Conceptual skills*. Imagine the futility of a ground control crew during space exploration if it should discover that the computer has gone dead in a launched vehicle. The situation is even more tragic when an organization discovers that one of its senior personnel officials is without conceptual skills. It means that the individual fails to comprehend the overall mission, organizational relationships, time frames, and the like. He lacks the capacity to adapt to new research findings,

new marketing and delivery strategies, new production technologies, and new labor force skill requirements. He is merely able to cope with the daily routine.

There are no new initiatives, no new directions, and no evidence of creativity or innovation. The ability to commit resources to long-range planning is missing, as is the ability to be a change agent in a dynamic environment. The individual takes hardened positions on policy issues, reflects little flexibility or pragmatism, and is unable to place himself in another's position. There is no ability to cope with a set of circumstances which differs from those generally encountered in the work. In some respects an individual without conceptual skills is like an individual who is mentally retarded.

5. *Management skills*. A senior official in a personnel department with substantive background and technical, human, and conceptual skills is still only about 60 percent of the whole person needed. Another 20 percent should be allocated to management skills. These are the skills that enable one to get things done through others. Luther Gulick said it well years ago when he coined the acronym POSDCORB for: planning, organizing, staffing, delegating, coordinating, reporting, and budgeting. The studies of Rensis Likert at the University of Michigan have identified the effective manager as the *linking pin* whose efforts make the difference between high and low productivity of the group being led.

The effective manager doesn't react; he causes things to happen that advance the goals and objectives of his organization in a manner that not only redounds to his organization's best interest but in so doing enables his subordinates to realize a sense of self-fulfillment.

6. *Communication skills*. Many good managers have effective communication skills—the ability to read, write, listen, speak, and lead meetings and conferences well—but some do

not. Therefore, it is worth breaking these skills out as a separate requirement to focus attention on them. Many individuals with effective human skills also have sharp communication skills, but some do not. For example, some people who interact well on a one-to-one basis strike out when asked to talk before a group or lead a conference.

The personnel department is heavily laden with paperwork of its own making, with circulating issuances from other parts of the organization, with laws, regulations, legal opinions, case histories, and the like. It is beset with people from every angle who need to be listened to. Without a doubt, no other department could have more need for communication skills of every variety.

Fortunately, there are proven methods for improving every communication skill. Reading courses can double the average reader's reading speed without any loss of comprehension. Writing courses can bring simplicity, strength, and readability to one's writing. Listening courses can improve one's recall ability. Speech courses can improve the organization and delivery of one's oral presentations. Conference leadership courses can make a great difference in the outcome of a meeting or conference.

It would be short-sighted for any personnel department not to invest in refresher training in communications for its first team. To the extent that it can make initial selections of individuals who already have real strength in this skill area, it should do so.

The Fixed-Tour-of-Duty Concept

Owners of professional sport teams have apparently learned that a coaching contract for a fixed tour of duty is desirable. They do not hire coaches for life or even for an indefinite period during which a winning record is maintained. When the coach has a sustained losing streak, or falls into bad repute with the players or the host city fans, his contract may not be renewed, and it may even be bought up before its expiration date. This is the system which should be seriously considered for the personnel department's first team.

Take a few more analogies. The local school principal may suffer severe damage to his image by a few untoward incidents at the school. Parents, teachers, and students alike may lose respect for the principal and cease to be supportive. A fixed-tour (rotational) system is a painless remedy. The same case can be made for having the local church minister on a fixed tour. I once knew a minister with an open-ended tour of duty at a local church who continued there for over 25 years as church attendance declined from a high of 1,000 to less than 200 even though the community remained relatively stable. The congregation could not bring itself to fire the minister, and he held on until he was retirable and had a second career opportunity in hand. Community-owned swimming pool associations have learned that a fixed-tour contract is the wisest course of action, for some managers click with the patrons and some do not.

One should also consider the fixed tour of duty in relation to the projected term of office of the corporate head of a private firm or the political administrator of a public agency. Such leadership obviously does not settle in for a lifetime or an indefinite period of good behavior. These leaders know that they are in place for a more or less fixed term such as two, four, or eight years. They enter upon duty with a "new broom" in the form of goals and objectives which have been fashioned during their dialog with the constituencies to whom they intend to be responsive and accountable. Too often they have to rely on a personnel department staffed from the top down with "lifers."

It is my thesis that the corporate head or the political administrator should have the option of naming his personnel director, for a fixed tour of duty, and that the personnel director in turn should have the same option with respect to his or her senior staff. Admittedly, such a plan has its complications in any tremendously large organization which considers itself a single employer. Nevertheless, such organizations should be able to work out a system of retreat rights or a senior executive corps with transfer rights from one branch of the parent establishment to another. Hiring controls can be imposed on organizational elements until the individuals in the reserve corps ranks have been absorbed. Also, the seniority, retirement service accrual, and other fringe benefit entitlements of the senior personnel staff need to be protected if the fixed-tour-of-duty concept is implemented.

Primary Source of Candidates

Personnel departments are strong advocates, and rightly so, of promotions-from-within programs. There is no better place in my judgment to start such programs than at the top of the department itself, with the understanding that the competitive area is the entire organization to be served by the personnel department. Given my list of six basic competencies, the field of choice is limited to individuals who have knowledge and experience in a substantive field and skills in five specific areas.

As stated earlier, the corporate head or the political administrator should be in a position to assemble a first team to run the personnel department for a tour of duty that more or less coincides with his own minimum expected term of office. They are definitely *not* to be political appointments based on partisan considerations. Instead, it is a matter of affording the responsible head of an organization and his immediate circle of advisers the right to pick a senior staff for the personnel department who can be counted on, without fail, to help them in every way possible deliver on his goals and objectives.

The primary source is not just line operations employees. Conceivably, some very worthy candidates with the six competencies can be found in staff positions. The critical point is that there should be no compromise on the six competencies. Here are some guidelines that I would use in winnowing final choices out of the field of candidates.

Experience mix. Give preference to individuals who have had the best balance of experience. Progressively responsible assignments in line, staff, field, and headquarters locations (sequence not critical) is the optimum mix. Orderly mobility and diversification accelerates growth and development. The "spiral staircase" model is superior to the "elevator shaft" model for this purpose.

Maturity. There are many roles in our society which seem to demand a good measure of maturity. Have you ever seen an exceptionally young or exceptionally old baseball umpire, commercial aircraft captain, surgeon, or chief of police? These and many other assignments demand just the right amount of maturity, and I believe the first team in the personnel department should be added to such ranks. These jobs require not only knowledge, skills, and abilities, but also poise, rhythm, and decisiveness. The candidates must be persons who instill confidence on the part of everyone affected by their actions. This is not to say that selection of the first team must always be governed by age. Some will have reached the stage of maturity sooner chronologically than others.

Ethnic, minority, and sex considerations. Selecting the best qualified person available for each place on the senior staff is the best guideline. However, other factors being more or less equal, there will be organizations that consistently or at specific phases of their life history need personnel department officials of a particular ethnic background. Women should be in key personnel positions in numbers roughly proportionate to their numbers in the labor force of the organization. Balance and representativeness are the two critical factors. For example, an organization with a labor force of 90 percent women is not going to be very happy with a personnel department with only males in its senior staff positions.

Energy. The first-team jobs in the personnel department are very demanding. These are not assignments for energyless, fragile people. It is difficult to see how a moonlighter with a second job or heavy outside commitments of any kind can do justice to his personnel department work. This is not to say that one should not continue to be active in relevant professional circles; but teaching three nights a week or working a full-time second job on weekends would be bad judgment.

Commitments. You need certain philosophical commitments to be an effective first-team member of a personnel department. You need to feel that human resources are the most vital of all resources at work in building the enterprise and ensuring its continuity of operations. You need to have certain perceptions with respect to the international scene. Obviously, the success or failure of the American economy is now linked inseparably with the economies of other nations. You need a fundamental commitment to such concepts as human rights, freedom of information, and equal opportunities in education, employment, and housing. You need genuine compassion and understanding of people as individuals and their need to have incentives, security, recognition, and redress of grievances.

Continuing growth and development. The tour of duty for the top team should be perceived by both the selecting officials and the selectee as a logical building block in the continuing growth and development of the team members. This assignment should not be regarded by either party as the end of the line or one that will be so image-tarnishing that further progress will be impossible without resigning and going outside.

First-team members should perceive their tour in the personnel department as an opportunity to gain real insights into the management and development of human resources. They can take back from the personnel department to the setting from which they came perspectives which will make them ambassadors for enlightened, integrated personnel administration. They should gain a good measure of self-renewal from the pressures of their substantive fields. In brief, the tour of duty in the personnel department should be a constructive and purposeful building block in their growth and development, and on their return to their fields of specialty they should be capable of moving to a higher performance plateau.

Secondary Sources of Candidates

The primary source of candidates for the first-team positions in the personnel department may not always yield a single candidate who measures well against the six-competencies test. What then? There are a number of auxiliary sources to which selecting officials might turn if they accept the view set forth in this chapter, namely, that the search is for someone to fill a fixed-tour assignment, with six basic competencies and certain other attributes. Here are several secondary sources that appeal to me.

Cooperative education institutions. Since the turn of the century, an extensive network of institutions of higher learning in the United States has managed learning systems that rotate the student between the campus and the world of work. If they believe in this system for students, they must be sympathetic to it for faculty members. Many business and industry enterprises already have well-established relationships with these "co-op" institutions. It would be a logical extension of this relationship for companies to negotiate reimbursable loans of professors or other appropriate arrangements. Some professors might be encouraged to do an extended sabbatical in a personnel department role.

Management consultants. This is a rich source of talent, because these are people who have been exposed to human resources problems in a diverse collection of enterprises. They have traced organizational successes and failures to people performance and the leadership element. A personnel department tour is a fine opportunity for individuals with a substantial background in management consulting (problem solving) to institutionalize whatever permanently useful generalizations they have gleaned.

Second-career people. Our society seems to be moving steadily toward acceptance of the proposition that "old Turks" should not be relegated to rocking chairs the minute they are eligible for first-career retirement. It has long been my conviction that financially independent people in our labor force may well be the only independent thinkers and nonconformists we have left. Since second-career people presumably are financially less dependent than first-career people, they may have that extra dimension—a seventh competency. This is a growing pool in our national inventory of human resources and should not be overlooked as a secondary source.

Management ranks. It would be remiss to overlook the management ranks themselves for possible choices to fill the first-team positions. Planned mobility is one of the finest people development strategies. The many facets of management, including personnel administration itself, should be screened for individuals who meet the tests set forth above.

The Selection Process

Careful recruitment and selection is hard work. It requires a series of deliberate, painstaking steps and cool judgment. Multiple judgment is safer than the judgment of any one individual. My experience indicates that the one-to-one interview is hardly any better as a selection device than the toss of a coin, and furthermore that the process of selection cannot be hurried.

A good way to begin is by designating a search committee. The committee should have available an executive secretary to coordinate its operations and manage its communications and records. The personnel director may want to use the search committee that facilitated his own selection or a new one to help select his senior staff. The personnel director should nominate and the personnel director's superior officer should confirm the selection of the personnel director's senior staff.

The search committee will probably need a whole series of meetings. Depending on the size of the field, it may wish to reduce the number of candidates to manageable proportions by the group oral examination. This is a method of screening four or five candidates at a time, using issues that stimulate dialog among the candidates while panelists observe the candidate interaction from the sidelines and weigh their strengths and weaknesses.

The screening by a search committee is but a first step in a thorough selection process. The finalists should be given an opportunity to observe, confer on, and read relevent materials about the work of the personnel department. A detailed position description, current organization charts, policy manuals, digests of laws and regulations, labor–management contracts, significant court actions, and federal, state, and local government requirements are examples of appropriate materials for their perusal. The selecting official may want to invite the finalists to a retreat for a get-acquainted session, and it would be well to include spouses in the invitation.

In filling key positions, we are inclined to have "full field" investigations made to resolve security and job suitability questions. This can leave a gaping hole in our investigation, especially if a single interviewer and a few vouchered references are substituted for the selection panel system. A sad approach to the selection process can often lead to a sad final choice. And, unfortunately, whereas hiring can be accomplished in hours, it may take months or years to fire an incompetent or unsuitable individual.

STEP 3: REFORMING THE PERSONNEL DEPARTMENT'S PRESENCE

Years ago, my economics professor instilled a fundamental principle of economics in my thinking. It had to do with delicatessens. My professor assured his class that consumers will continue to patronize convenience goods stores, such as the neighborhood delicatessen, and pay more for items they buy there.

The professor was right. I have watched other businesses come and go while the delicatessens I have known continued year after year selling convenience goods at premium prices. In fact, if you look around, you will find whole chains of stores trading on that economics principle.

My marketing professor also taught that there is a preferred side of the road for certain kinds of stores. Food stores, he said, should be on the right-hand side of the road for people returning from work in their automobiles. The professor must have been right, for I have never found a successful grocery store on the left-hand side of the road as I returned home from work.

What do delicatessens and sides of the road have to do with personnel offices? Let me explain. Many of the personnel offices I have known have deliberately selected a place of business away from the mainstream of traffic. They have sought out the quiet retreat on an upper floor or in a separate annex as if they needed the atmosphere of a research library. They lacked a *presence* near the operating people. This means that supervisors and managers, and employees generally, have to make a special trip to see the personnel people about a personnel problem.

The business community has demonstrated so conclusively the merit of decentralized services, in terms of both physical presence and authority to act, that I should think personnel departments would get the cue and take their services to the work scene. In brief, they need to create a presence near the "market" for their services.

Location of Personnel Department Headquarters

The headquarters of the personnel department can be an exception to the presence rule. The headquarters location should be controlled by the location of the enterprise's headquarters. The personnel director is an integral part of the senior staff of the enterprise. As such, he or she needs a position which will facilitate close collaboration with other top management officials. "Presence" for the headquarters staff means close proximity to the focal point for policy formulation. The management principle of span of control dictates that those within easy access of the chief executive officer are more likely to participate in decisions than those who are remote.

Everything the state of the art in communications has to offer should be put to work in linking the staff of the personnel department headquarters with its decentralized counterparts. When the linkage is by memorandum, communication is slow, cumbersome, and expensive. Moreover, the personnel office may well have lost its opportunity to be an active partner in solving operating problems. Delays in reaching the scene may seem like procrastination.

Some personnel departments are apprehensive about the possibility of being summoned by the chief executive officer to explain a personnel action or to outline a personnel strategy to meet some new operating requirements. Apprehensive personnel offices prefer nonparticipatory roles. Interoffice buzzers and telephone jingles can unsettle them.

Location of Operating Personnel Offices

The operating personnel office has several different clienteles. These include job applicants, supervisors and managers, executives, and rank and file personnel. How can it possibly be optimally located to serve all these groups efficiently? The answer is that it cannot if it insists on presenting itself as one consolidated whole at a single location. Nevertheless, we as members of personnel groups persist in keeping ourselves collected together as if we need the mutual security of each other's presence. Here are some guidelines which I would prefer to see us use in locating our several local outposts.

1. Posture

The point has already been made that the personnel department and its counterpart local units must be a genuine *service arm* of management. This means that their posture is one of "service with a smile" and "the customer is always right." Some of its services should be so efficiently organized that the client gets instant, on-the-spot help. Other services that require more time should be delivered in an orderly manner within a reasonable time.

2. *Mobility and Flexibility*

These are the keys to delivering on the pledge of efficient service with a smile. Suppose that as a matter of policy a television station were to insist on making the principals in all newsworthy events come to its main studio for televising. Mobile crews and isolated television cameras would not be a part of its style. How long would such a station survive? The personnel office, like the television station, needs a base of operations. This represents its production planning capability, its means of coordination, continuity, documentation, and related processes. Here are some other ways to deploy the personnel staff with mobility and flexibility.

Teams in residence. One personnel office may serve only one large operating department or one of its divisions. It cannot serve its client adequately from a fixed location, no more than the central personnel department headquarters can. Further, we have a strong tendency to arrange our personnel staffs both organizationally and physically into "watertight compartments," with referral from one set of specialists to another being minimal. A problem presented by operating people to any particular group of personnel specialists is dealt with unilaterally.

Why not blunt these tendencies by (1) stationing a "team in residence" in the quarters of a major client, and (2) forming the team with representatives of the personnel specialties in greatest demand? For example, one team in residence might consist of an organization and job analyst, a placement officer, a classification analyst, and an employee relations officer. The team should be seated in one large room with movable partitions to encourage communication among the team members. The team composition may vary from team to team and even within the same team, depending upon the personnel department emphasis and the current operating requirements of the client.

Mobile teams. The decentralized personnel office will doubtless find peaks and valleys in the demand for its services. If the key is mobility and flexibility, it has to have a mechanism for responding to peak demands, just as a local school system must respond to classroom planning problems due to dynamic conditions in high-rise housing policy. This policy can impact on classroom needs faster than the school boards can afford to build, enlarge, or close schools. Consequently, they may have to hold a few mobile classrooms in readiness to move into place to accommodate overloads in any given school district. The personnel office can use this principle by identifying members of a mobile team in advance and having the team on call to meet urgent demands for personnel services.

Traffic stream desks. We see flight insurance company desks in busy airports where the potential customers are preparing for departure. We see military service recruiter desks in shopping centers, where they can have presence and visibility to potential recruits. But how many personnel office desks have you seen in the traffic stream either within their own establishment or alongside the insurance desk and the military recruiter desk at outside locations?

Again, I have to conclude that we personnel people have been hiding out from our clientele. Do you know of any individual in the entire labor force who does not have some questions he or she would like answered authoritatively by a personnel representative?

You may reason that such a desk would be a magnet for many idle questions and would soon come to the same unhappy end as the phone company's information number (411) did; that is, that the personnel office would have to set up a public relations program to discourage the use of the desk, and even institute a fee-for-service scheme to make users feel it in the pocketbook. That remains to be seen on a cost/benefit analysis basis.

What would the personnel desk attendant do? A well-trained individual's range of duties and responsibilities is limited only by the full scope of personnel administration and one's imagination. For example, he or she could:

Accept applications for posted vacancies.
Answer questions on qualification standards for specific positions.
Explain to employees how career ladders work.
Answer questions on position classification standards.
Interpret the leave regulations and other fringe benefits.
Identify individuals in the personnel office to whom one should go for specific kinds of help, say, to file a grievance.
Distribute fact sheets and newsletters as a means of continuing orientation.
Accept beneficial suggestions and assist anyone requesting help in completing the suggestion form.
Explain the incentives system.
Accept registration cards for car-pooling and other common-need services.
Refer employees to the credit union.
Accept contributions to worthy causes in which the enterprise cooperates by soliciting funds.
Distribute literature about recreational opportunities sponsored by the employer.

Task groups. There will be occasions when the personnel office cannot independently solve the client's problem. A joint-venture effort is required. My experience indicates that standing committees are frequently ineffective, because the problem may outlast some of the ablest members' availability for committee duty. A task group can tackle a specific segment of the larger problem, using a definite beginning and ending date as a time frame. Then a second task group can move the issue further by undertaking another segment of the work. The personnel input to the task group effort could, of course, be by either a resident or mobile team as described above.

Task groups have many incidental advantages. They are a vehicle for identifying personnel with exceptional qualifications. They provide a new dimension of motivation and reward for those who become involved. The personnel department can interpret its programs and enlist greater support and interaction through task groups than through unilateral action. They spread the cost of doing business over both the personnel group and the client, thus giving the client a sense of investment and participation in the resolution of his own personnel needs.

Contractual services. Many organizations act too hastily by contracting out their in-house management responsibilities. They can end up educating the contractor and buying back their own knowledge and experience—at a price they need not pay. Yet, there are times when contracting a piece of the action to a reliable outside organization is a sensible thing to do.

The contract should not be drawn cavalierly. The scope of work element needs precise language. Several bidders with capability of a known level should be invited to bid. The contract needs to be monitored carefully. The contractual relationship should, if possible, be used as a growth experience for the personnel staff as well as a way of meeting the client's operating needs.

How should contractors be used? This will vary widely depending on the enterprise engaging the contractor. In one situation, an employment agency may be engaged to help meet a massive recruitment need. In another, a management consulting firm may be engaged to help in a major reorganization. Or a public relations firm may be engaged to assist the employer in maintaining its public image during a particularly difficult contract renegotiation when a strike may occur.

Top management liaison. The span-of-control principle is relevant to the issue of if, when, and how the operating personnel office participates in policy formulation at the top management level of its clients. We can take another leaf from the book of American free private enterprise. How do business concerns make their concerns and recommendations known to legislators? Through paid representatives who are known as lobbyists. There are some bad lobbyists, I suppose, but the lobbyists I have known are as nice as any other group of people. The point is that they have a *presence* in places where it counts and they evidently are rather effective in presenting the case of their clients.

The personnel office needs to have a presence in places where its clients do business. Meetings, conferences, luncheons, retreats, seminars, and conventions are logical places for personnel representatives to appear. The representative should be as smooth as the skilled lobbyist. Such a strategy could even lead to the phenomenon of "preventive personnel administration."

3. Communications

The personnel office is a poor place to economize on communications systems. Literally every employee, countless outsiders such as job applicants, other employers, regulatory agencies, credit bureaus, police departments and other investigative networks, and diverse other interests need to communicate with the personnel office.

Truck drivers have their citizens' band radios and other

radio systems in their cabs. Taxis, appliance repair people, utility companies, and numerous other public service enterprises have instant two-way communication. I strongly advocate that personnel offices consider beefing up their communications capability. Here are some thoughts on what they could do.

Communications advice. Any communications expert familiar with the state of the art can prescribe a system tailored to the real needs of any personnel office. The mistake many organizations make when they sense the need for more communications capability is to call the telephone company to send over one of its engineers to look the situation over. Telephones are obviously just one way we communicate today.

Telephones. The telephone capability of many personnel offices is about what one would have expected at the turn of the century. You ring a number and you often get a busy signal because, perhaps, "Mary" is on the party line having a chat with "Johnny."

Multimedia communications. The spoken word may be the fastest means of communication, but a multimedia system is probably the best for a personnel office that genuinely wants to communicate. For example, the teletypewriter has made an invaluable contribution to communication in the United States for decades, but I have never seen a teletypewriter system in a personnel office. Why not? It affords a fast, concise, and written means of communication. Transportation people have long recognized its value and they routinely issue tickets worth substantial sums of money while the customer waits only minutes at a remote location, such as the office of his travel agent in his own neighborhood shopping center. Sophisticated personnel offices should seriously consider teletype equipment as a means of communication.

Since the CB radio is apparently here to stay, it might also be considered. And there are numerous other systems.

Written word. The written word can still be a fast means of communication for any personnel office willing to change its stifling writing style. The bureaucratic and legalistic memorandum type of writing is the prevailing style in personnel offices. A daily or weekly "news flash" summary with two or three lines per item could keep operating officials informed of the happenings on the personnel front. Another worthy possibility is a monthly or quarterly report done largely with simple graphics—charts and graphs (supporting data annexed)—to show trends in such areas as turnover, new hires, demographic mix, grievances filed and heard, and promotions from within.

4. Office Layout

A poor, ill-equipped personnel office layout can be uninviting—the kind of place that makes one feel uncomfortable and not ever want to stop in again except out of sheer necessity. Such unpleasantness is far from being compatible with the proposition set forth earlier, namely, that the posture of the personnel office should be one of "service with a smile" and "the customer is always right." Here are some suggestions.

Presentability. Any good architect or facilities planner knows that space can be made inviting, and kept so, at a cost no more than that required to maintain a drab space. Paint, carpeting, and light are the critical ingredients, and they are relatively inexpensive.

Informality. Informality should be another key factor in planning the office layout. Every room in a personnel office tends to look as formal as a courtroom, with the judge's high-back chair, an executive desk separating the employee from the personnel representative, and other amenities that too often symbolize authority and control rather than a friendly counselor.

Color dynamics, indirect lighting, some well-chosen wall hangings, and a few potted plants are further suggested as a way of making personnel space presentable and inviting. Some color-coordinated and simple furniture completes the scene.

Clustering. The suggestion made above for clustering certain specialists of the personnel group into interdisciplinary teams should, if possible, be instituted in the design of the layout. Personnel specialists should not operate like "Judge Bean" in Texas folklore, who deals with a case as if he were a one-person Supreme Court without benefit of lower courts or other justices with whom to interact in reaching a position on the issue. It has long seemed reasonable to me to cluster together a team of specialists from the several personnel disciplines (preferably employment, classification, and employee relations) in order to induce a more cooperative approach to problem solving. When people work in close proximity, they get to know each other much better, and the chances of cooperation are enhanced.

Semiprivacy. There are ways, short of walling off the space from floor to ceiling, of creating semiprivate space for members of personnel teams even though they are clustered. The business world manages to do it even in banking, where individuals must bare the facts of their financial lives in order to obtain loans. If they can do it, personnel offices can.

Functional features. Another thought worth mentioning here is that personnel space should be made functional. There are many marvelous audiovisual devices on the market. But where are the A/V devices stationed? Too often you will find them in a conference room, training room, or locked storeroom—idle. Why can't a few of these devices be on indefinite loan to the personnel office? A small A/V device that normally serves as a teaching machine in a training room could be used by the employment office to give a brief orientation on the mission of the enterprise to one applicant, or a glimpse of the actual work environment in a particular line of work to another.

I once knew a school system whose teacher recruitment teams used three-dimensional (stereo) slides very effectively in their spring canvass for the best candidates at teacher training institutions. A/V devices could instantly portray organizational relationships, career ladders, salary scale and fringe benefits, the promotion-from-within system, highlights of labor–management contracts, the grievance procedure, and other matters of interest to both job applicants and employees. Microfiche has probably not been applied in the personnel office to the extent it could be applied effectively.

In summary, the personnel department and its counterpart local units should come out of their cloistered places and create a *presence* in every way possible. That presence should make it easy for the personnel people to serve top management, line operations and other staff groups, employees generally, and job applicants. They can do this best, in my judgment, by establishing a posture of service, by organizing and managing their activities with much mobility and flexibility, by exploiting the state of the art in communications technology, and by working in appealing and functional office settings.

STEP 4: INCREASING THE PERSONNEL DEPARTMENT'S RESPONSIVENESS

Ideally, at this point, the chief executive officer has declared the personnel director to be a corporate officer of "cabinet rank." The "first team" has been put in place through collaboration between these two individuals. That team is aware of its identity: they are operating people on consignment to the personnel department for a specific tour of duty to serve top management by helping operating people and other staff groups, employees generally, and job applicants with their personnel problems.

Each member of the team has been carefully selected. Each will have been measured against the "six competencies" standard suggested earlier and have some additional special attributes. They have a positive attitude on service to their clients. Their local counterpart staffs will be deployed with a high degree of mobility and flexibility. These staffs are ready to function from inviting, functional quarters with ample communications capability.

With all this, what else could be needed? In a word, *responsiveness.* The challenge is to accomplish the maximum good for the greatest number of current and prospective employees within a fixed tour of duty. More specifically, the issue is how to deliver the necessary quality services, using a staff that is fully conditioned and ready for action. Each member of the personnel staff must be intelligent, highly trained, self-disciplined, alert, and properly motivated.

To meet such a challenge is not easy. I believe it takes some imagination and nonconformity. The freshening effect of rotational tours on the personnel department's first team in itself should go a long way toward establishing new response patterns. My purpose in this chapter is to try to open new vistas for individuals who may themselves be first-team members some day, as well as people who are in a position to influence the thinking of personnel department officials.

Backstopping Support

The goals of any mission are not assured without good backstopping support. Personnel offices are no exception and should not try to go it alone. Here are several readily available sources of backstopping support.

The library system. The United States has a remarkable network of library systems. They serve every age group from preschoolers to senior citizens, the blind, and individuals living in remote places. And yet, I have known countless personnel people who would never use the library even if they had to walk through it to get to the rest room.

Modern library systems have highly developed technologies that enable them to retrieve and duplicate relevant research material. Some of their holdings are in audiovisual format. Libraries usually have linkage with each other, so if your local library does not have a source item, it can borrow and have it available within a few hours.

Some libraries will do some preliminary research for its patrons by screening its holdings and making a selected bibliography. Most librarians are anxious to be helpful by putting their professional skills to work, for the custodial tasks of the library are not exciting.

Professional societies. One test of the degree to which we have managed to professionalize personnel administration, I believe, is the extent to which we have involved ourselves in, and profitably use, our professional societies. Superficial involvement, such as attendance at a monthly luncheon to socialize or run for an office to gain personal visibility, should not count. The great majority of all personnel offices would probably fail this professionalization test.

The professional society is presumably the memory bank of what has been learned to date in a given field of work. The paid staff of a professional society is there to assist members. From their unique communications vantage point, they are in a position to know where new frontiers are being etched. They can be the switchboard-type linkage among members faced with similar problems. They either have resource material, or they are likely to know of good sources. They know who the real leaders in particular specialties are. They are in a position to help with conceptual planning, to evaluate commercial systems and devices, and to identify available candidates for employment or technical assistance.

The galaxy of professional societies is relatively unexplored by personnel offices, even though the personnel office's exploration task is vastly easier than the scientist's. I say we should get busy and tap this source of backstopping support.

Academe. Urban areas are studded with colleges and universities dispensing continuing education. The student body is almost synonymous with the adult population itself, as a high percentage of adults pursue courses for occupational or recreational reasons. Many instructors teach by the case history method, encouraging their students to do practical observation and before-and-after analysis of institutional change. We in personnel should cooperate with these academe-based projects. Students presumably have no vested interest in the outcome of studies, as subordinates in an organization do, so their work should be more objective.

Many professors are constantly searching for ways and means of testing new hypotheses in order to advance some of their own research and writing objectives. They are pleased when they can influence policies and practices of the business and industrial community of which they are a part. Interaction between us and the professors can be mutually rewarding as well as a rich source of backstopping support for our personnel offices. Should it ever become necessary for our personnel office to contract with a local educational institution for research or consultation, we will have some background on its capability.

The marketplace. The marketplace is a marvelous source of new ideas and backstopping support. Sales people delight in consigning their equipment for trial use. They are good catalysts, since they move about in their sales territory and see the results of new methods and devices. They will gladly stage demonstrations for personnel people and operations personnel. Sales people are usually current on recent and pending changes in legislation and regulations. Sales representatives of reputable companies have always served my professional interests well.

Public agencies. Personnel people have a wide range of public agencies to turn to for backstopping support. Such agencies have diverse interests, including employment, unemployment, labor–management difficulties, health, job training, wages and hours, Social Security, environmental protection, retirement programs, civil rights, freedom of information, privacy, and workers' compensation. Granted that dealing with public agencies can be cumbersome, any employer is shortchanging itself to stand aloof to public agency services.

Model Building

One of the most impressive field trips one can take is a visit to a U.S. Department of Agriculture experimental station, such as the one at Beltsville, Maryland. Here one can see experiments that have been in progress for years in such scientific fields as animal breeding, milk production, crops, grasses, insecticides, fertilizers, and implements. When a piece of new knowledge reaches the marketable stage, the station calls in interested commercial-market representatives, demonstrates its findings, and invites applications for authorization to begin production and distribution. This is a choice example of frutiful cooperation between the public and private sectors in the general interest.

The personnel department is in a position, with all the backstopping support it has, to emulate this relationship. Enterprises of varying sizes and geographic dispersion could provide the setting for experimentation and innovation in such processes as recruitment, selection, placement, supervision, performance standards, incentives, performance appraisal, and organization. Perhaps the most serious charge that can be leveled at us in personnel administration is the sameness of our programs and our failure to try new systems and methods in a scientific way. Responsiveness to operating needs should, in my judgment, be based on a certain amount of pragmatism and experimentation.

Essentially, the central personnel department, with the help of its local branches, can orchestrate improvements in methodology. One local personnel office can be trying out one new method while another personnel office is testing another method. The results of central monitoring and analysis can be summarized periodically in reports to all interested personnel offices in the enterprise. Overall policies and standards can be adjusted accordingly.

The scale of research and model building need not be very large. The important thing is to have some efforts going in the organization at all times to advance knowledge in personnel administration, and to make sure that such research, regardless of scale, is conceptually well planned, organized, monitored, and reported.

Dialogs with Labor

"We have met the enemy and they is us," says Pogo of the comics. This may well apply to the way in which we sometimes neglect our relations with labor groups. The roots of labor's suspicion, strife, choice of demagogic leadership at times, and other unbecoming behavior patterns are fed, in part, by management's failure to be responsive when it desperately needs to be responsive. Since our personnel department carries much of the burden of management's responsiveness, we need to find ways to stimulate and improve our response pattern.

Granted that labor's appraisal of management may be

harsh, we are obliged to try to comprehend our standing. Conflicts may be caused by a total void in top leadership, greed of owners, arrogance of management, lack of humanitarianism, secrecy, failure to update technology or human resources, failure to use participative management styles, or any combination of these factors.

Some of our personnel departments believe that the best posture is to deal with labor leaders only when a grievance or strike occurs and at contract negotiation time. This, in my judgment, is a poor stance. Labor people are almost invariably well informed, committed, and capable of presenting an impressive case on behalf of their members. They cannot always be wrong. Obviously, the more differences can be settled at the source, the less ground there will be for major labor–management confrontations.

The results of continuing dialogs with labor by the personnel department can be quietly translated into programmatic changes. The training and development staff should know what to emphasize in their development of supervisors and managers. As labor sees that changes are made, it may cultivate better relations and soften the bite in periods of labor–management confrontation.

Keeping Current

Professional sports teams scout their competition to make sure that there are no strategies in use that they are inexperienced in coping with. There should be some such system by which personnel departments can see other personnel systems in action. All of us in personnel administration have doubts at times as to whether or not the literature in the field is current and authoritative. Much of it is written by a small but articulate group.

More specifically, how do we know when to update ourselves and our subordinate staff members? The continuing-education marketplace is full of course offerings, but personnel managers need a yardstick for determining individual needs and for timing development experiences. Making wise choices among such diverse offerings is also difficult. Courses that use workshop and practical observation as learning modes are, in my experience, more fruitful than straight lecture courses.

In trying to keep current, one should not overlook the possibility of using the telephone or simply going across the city (or around the corner) to a professional colleague's place of business to find out how he does things. Classrooms have no monopoly on knowledge. Growth takes an open mind, willingness to try new approaches, and absolute honesty in weighing the results.

One other point is worth mentioning as a means of keeping current in order to be more responsive. Some of us wear blinders that shut out progress of other nations in specialized fields such as personnel administration. There are several professional societies with an international dimension in personnel administration. The cultural attachés of foreign embassies in the United States can be very helpful. The U.S. State Department, through its ambassadors and overseas posts, can gather information. Commercial interests abroad are a rich source. Many universities with consultative and exchange programs abroad can help. It is safe to say that no personnel department really interested in a study of comparative personnel administration methods is without sources of data.

Self-Appraisal

Television programs live or die from consumer preference polls run by such rating services as Nielsen's. If we really want our departments to be useful to client groups, why shouldn't we use this same principle? There are several angles from which appraisal data can be gathered. On-board employees are one. People who become turnover statistics are another. Supervisors and managers are a third. Operating officials and top management executives are a fourth.

Even a self-appraisal by the personnel staff itself can be constructive. Collection of performance data on the department should be guided by an expert in survey design, and the resulting data should be impartially analyzed and reported. Many large organizations have in-house capabilities for making such studies.

There is another way to take a reading on personnel department performance that strikes me as relevant: the board-of-visitors concept from academe. The visiting board need not be staffed fully with personnel experts. It could be a mix of in-house individuals who have diverse interests in the total productive effort of the enterprise. One or more outside personnel specialists might be added. The board of visitors need not be regarded as a hostile force. It can lend credence to some thinking of the personnel department that has fallen on deaf ears in top management circles. It may also support operating program needs the personnel department has been slow to embrace.

Health maintenance organizations (HMOs), which are relatively new on the American scene except in scattered locations, are now stressing *quality of care* as one of their major goals. To measure their progress, they are developing data from members who receive service benefits. The time has come, in my judgment, for personnel departments to become more quality-of-care oriented. They have much in common with HMOs, and the success or failure of personnel department programs may indirectly affect the workload of HMOs. Knowing how well they are hitting the mark of human resources needs can improve the rate and quality of response.

Institutional Memory

Incoming chief executive officers are sometimes faced with having to retain one or more members of the outgoing executive's senior staff in order to have even a semblance of an institutional memory. The outgoing team may have been discredited in the eyes of the staff it directed. One reason for failure may have been its neglect of records management responsibilities. When an incoming team cannot make heads or tails of the records, it has to decide issues and specific cases without benefit of the historical evolution of a program or practice.

If management is ever to approach the precision level of science it has to adopt the clinical approach to recordation. A personnel office cannot begin to be intelligently responsive until it disciplines itself severely about records. Desks and personnel specialists have to be freely interchangeable; unless they are, the record-keeping and records management systems and human practices are deficient.

I am convinced that this objective can be attained without making robots out of personnel people. Doctors, dentists, attorneys, engineers, and many other professionals log their encounters, and they do it smoothly and with quiet efficiency. It is doubtful that those of us in personnel administration who resist this discipline will ever truly become professional in our approach or responsive to the needs we profess to serve.

Unwavering Integrity

On many occasions I have observed operating officials exploiting their personnel office by insisting that it do things to people that they (the operating officials) didn't have the courage to do themselves. This can involve any aspect of personnel administration, and the practice is without regard to sex, age group, ethnic background, national origin or experience level of the operating official. This is an abominable practice. Personnel officials who yield to such pressures are no better than operating officials who try exploitation.

Equally lacking in integrity is the personnel official who compromises personnel standards by responding affirmatively to inside or outside pressures to favor certain employees or job applicants because of kinship, politics, or affiliation with a special interest group. Under the system of selection recommended in this chapter for the senior staff of a personnel department, the personnel official on whom the primary responsibility for action rests can simply resign his tour of duty and, at the earliest practicable date, revert to the operations post where he has retreat rights.

Running errands, so to speak, for interests that run counter to the principles for which a personnel department stands is time-consuming and enervating. It can deprive personnel officials of the time they need to respond to valid claims on their time. It can rob them of the self-esteem and identity they need to do the job that demands the intelligent application of talent, skill, and unwavering integrity.

Chapter 5

Stage Two: Improving the Scope and Quality of Personnel Service

STAFF MEMBERS of the central personnel department and its local branches are not expected to sit at their desks like granite statuary. There is a ready demand for our services. The secret is in how to offer more than knee-jerk reaction. I believe we need a well-conceived plan of action in order to cope with the wide spectrum of organizational and human resources needs. This chapter highlights my thinking on how we can be constructive and useful in helping others cope with such needs.

ADVISING MANAGEMENT ON ORGANIZATIONAL PATTERNS

This should not be an off-limits issue for the personnel department. Management analysts, budget analysts, industrial engineers, controllers, and assorted others in the management family have had the ear of top management a great deal more than we have on matters of organization. We need to be heard on this vital issue which affects the qualification requirements, standards of performance, morale, and productivity of employees generally. For example, we may be feeding new employees into a two-boss situation, situations where responsibility exceeds authority, or impossible span-of-control relationships. The revolving door of turnover will probably take a heavy toll and leave everyone concerned very frustrated.

The best rationale for having the personnel staff provide staff support and advice to top management on organization matters seems to me to be the inseparable linkage between organizational effectiveness and people potential and performance. We in personnel presumably are in closer touch with people in the organization than any other element of the organization is, from the time they become job applicants until they are separated from the rolls. While this cognizance may be minimal when individuals are at the lower levels of responsibility, it increases rapidly as they progress to supervisory, managerial, and executive levels. We have many more ways for monitoring their conduct and performance, their training, education and growth, and their participation in extra-duty activities such as hobbies and recreational and community interests.

MANPOWER PLANNING

As I have already indicated, it is my belief that manpower planning is a line function that can best be served by operating officials. We should contribute to the manpower planning process with all the data and technical advice and assistance we can furnish. For example, we personnel specialists have data on which to project retirement and routine turnover.

We can estimate recruitment and orientation time. We can forecast the time required to establish any new positions and complete the payroll procedures. We may have a better feel for the changes ahead in overall employment policy.

Operating officials are in a better position to judge such factors as social and economic conditions, changes in government standards, the impact of technology, marketing strategies, the impact of consumerism, and manpower implications of new products and services. These are the gut issues of manpower planning. For us in the personnel office to try to substitute our judgment for that of line officials is ludicrous.

We are in a position to study the dynamics of organizational change as we move individuals in and out of certain jobs. Some years ago, a national mail order and retail store chain was advocating and practicing "flat" organization, the chief advocate being the assistant chief executive for personnel administration. He claimed that only three or four persons were in the chain of command between the retail store clerk who sells an automobile tire to a customer and the president of the firm.

Bureaucracies like more pyramiding and totem pole effect in their organizational arrangements. I am confident that if the same clerk were transferred to a bureaucracy to sell tires, he would find a dozen or more people between him and the chief exectuive officer.

Can both styles be equally effective? I believe not, and therefore I believe we personnel specialists should be counseling management on how to organize according to the demonstrably better method.

We can develop other perceptions about organization, too. I have long held a bias against the use of deputies, that is, people who appear in the chain of command between the chief and managers who run operating groups. It insulates the chief, slows communication, breeds suspicion and jealousy, encourages "end runs" around the deputy, and wastes time and money by duplicating effort and slowing the decision process.

Some organizations vacillate from centralization to decentralization of authority, depending on where they get their advice on organization theory. Some practice geographic concentration, and others practice geographic dispersion. Some concentrate authority and responsibility in their line operations groups; others give a good measure of it to technical assistance groups in staff capacities. Some organizations keep static organizational formats for years; others are more sensitive to informal organization (people changes), economic forces, and the political winds.

It is my contention that all these organizations cannot be right at all times in their choices of organizational pattern; therefore, they should look first to in-house sources of advice on organization matters. Here, the personnel department is a logical source of expertise. Where it isn't, top management should make it one of its own high priorities to build such capability in the personnel department.

CLASSIFYING POSITIONS

Merit systems and the plea "equal pay for equal work" gave rise to position classification well over 50 years ago, especially in the public sector. The classification system in the federal civil service dates from 1923. There is no better foundation for a job-oriented career system in either the private or public sector than position classification. It involves the arrangement of jobs into groups or classes on the basis of duties, responsibilities, and qualification requirements. From this foundation, our work as personnel specialists is facilitated in formulating and administering standards of performance, employee training and career development requirements, incentives, promotion plans, compensation schedules, and procedures for investigating and settling grievances.

I am not a blind advocate of position classification. It has considerable merit wherever it is administered imaginatively and equitably. But therein lies the difficulty. There is much room for subjective action in determining position classification standards for each class, in analyzing and evaluating the duties of each position, and in the assignment of the position to a particular class and grade.

Unfortunately, position classifiers are human beings, and their own progress within the system weighs on the scales they use to measure the work of others. For example, I have known classifiers who were exceedingly conservative in evaluating clerical jobs, such as file clerk and fiscal clerk, but were liberal in evaluating professional positions such as economist and statistician. This was generally believed to be the case because the classifiers understood clerical work but had no feel for economics and statistics.

Another factor that gives me some pause about the position classification concept is referred to in position classification circles as "effect of incumbency." Classifiers imagine this phenomenon occurs with about the same infrequency as human twins. It just may be the other way around. How many people do you know who bring the identical background to comparable jobs and whose outputs in quantity, quality, and manner of performance are the same? Our whole military career system is built on the concept of "rank in the man." Under that plan, rank is determined through much greater emphasis on a multiple-judgment process than the grade of a person is determined under the "rank in the job" plans.

There are other significant exceptions to the equal pay for equal work concept. In the crafts, blue-collar workers negotiate wage contracts on the basis of prevailing locality rates and other factors. We are also seeing the use of bonus schemes being introduced into the pay plan for managers and executives to spur them on to better production results by such methods as weeding out marginal producers, taking new initiatives, working harder, and getting others to work harder.

The fact that position classification is not universally applied to all jobs in all enterprises and does not work flawlessly where it is applied should be a yellow light to all of us. Position classification is obviously not a cure-all. In selective situations where it has a reasonable chance of working well, I would offer these thoughts.

- Be extremely careful in the selection of position classifiers. The work is drudgery for many people, and it is a narrow specialty that offers limited career development opportunity. It takes a special mind disciplined for the analytical process. One of the best classifiers I have ever known was trained as a chemist. It takes special training and tremendous depth in the enterprise itself. Perhaps it should be treated as a "tour of duty" rather than a permanent placement. Why not consider individuals who have a rich background in the enterprise and who are in the last few years of their first career—a time, presumably, when they are not driven so hard by the get-ahead motive?
- Insist that position classification be a joint venture between operating personnel and the personnel office. This applies to both the development of classification standards and the determination of classes and grades.
- Force position classification to relate to the job analysis function. The personnel office should be doing this regularly for other reasons.
- Career patterns are paramount. Isolated jobs, regardless of how well they are described and classified, are meaningless unless they are an integral part of specific career patterns.

• The training and development and the career counseling service should keep all employees currently informed of their opportunities and responsibilities under the position classification system. For example, every employee should be entitled to a unit of instruction in how to prepare a position description.

• Position classification requires perpetual care and administration. It is often administered on a "grease-the-wheel-that-squeaks" basis. When inequities occur on this basis, loss of confidence in the system can spread rapidly.

SETTING PAY

Much of the social policy of our nation revolves around the amount of current income and anticipated future income the citizen should expect for his contribution to the gross national product. Grassroots pressures have mounted over the years and forced the Congress of the United States to legislate on maximum hours, income taxes, welfare assistance, unemployment income, Social Security, methods for resolving labor–management disputes over wages and benefits, workers' compensation, salaries, retirement plans, injury compensation of civilian and military employees, and a variety of related issues. State and local governments levy various kinds of taxes to ensure the continuity of community services.

All these manifestations of social policy can be reduced to a lowest common denominator, namely, that the majority of us believe that people are entitled to a living wage under our economic system and that they should be able to live out their lives without loss of dignity and self-esteem due to financial conditions over which they have no control. This proposition imposes upon all of us in personnel administration the obligation to see to it that pay and fringe benefits are set at a level and in a manner that will leave the worker with a feeling that both the process and the end result have been fair and just.

Public agencies generally publish salary schedules, by grade, and provide for periodic increments for employees with satisfactory performance. There may also be a provision for special increases for outstanding performance and beneficial suggestions. Private enterprises are more secretive on matters of pay. They tend to operate without published schedules, to negotiate individually with job candidates, and to distribute take-home pay in sealed envelopes. I believe these and other such practices are all a mistake. Secrecy breeds suspicion that management is rewarding its favorites and punishing its "whistle blowers" and others out of favor.

The responsibility for making local surveys to find out what is going on in the labor market should be diffused in a wage board. Some organizations are so secretive that they will not even share their pay data with another organization or with an impartial group that is serving as a clearinghouse. It would be in the interest of all concerned, for both public and private employers within a region, to share their pay data freely with a central clearinghouse. Comparability of pay for similar work is a worthy goal for all employers in a given region. It could reduce job-hopping, friction, loss of production time, and inflation.

The consumer price index (CPI) is a prodcut of scientifically proven statistical sampling formulas and survey methods. The federal government is guided by the CPI in adjusting pay, retirement, and Social Security stipends. The substandard living conditions of many poor and elderly people in our society are due in no small part to the fact that some employers in the private sector have not recognized the CPI and not pegged their own pension plans to the index, thus leaving a segment of the population with fixed retirement income of diminishing worth in an inflationary economy. Reportedly, some of these people have to turn to pet food and other substitutes for nutritionally sound diets. The worst effect of all, of course, is the damage to their self-esteem and dignity.

Granted that it is hard to determine the proper share of labor in the value of goods and services produced, the leadership of an organization should commit itself to making such a determination. Strikes, like wars, are a cruel way to settle differences.

A fine example of a constructive initiative taken jointly by management and labor occurred in 1948, when General Motors and the United Automobile Workers entered into an agreement with an unprecedented provision. It had two innovations: a cost-of-living escalator clause to protect real wages, and an "annual improvement factor" increase in real wages by an amount that was about equal in percentage to the long-term increase in the national private sector productivity per employee man-hour. The 1948 annual improvement clause, which has been continued in subsequent revisions of the agreement, reads:

> The annual improvement factor provided therein recognizes that a continuing improvement in the standard of living of employees depends upon technological progress, better tools, methods, process and equipment, and a cooperative attitude on the part of all parties in such progress. It further recognizes the principle that to produce more with the same amount of human effort is a sound economic and social objective.

Another approach to productivity sharing is known as the Scanlon Plan. Joseph N. Scanlon in the early 1940s proposed joint labor–management committees to solicit employee suggestions on how efficiency could be increased, production costs reduced, and waste eliminated. Benefits were to be shared through steady employment, higher wages, and better working conditions. His work was continued at M.I.T., where Scanlon was a member of the industrial relations staff helping companies and their unions or non-unionized employees to introduce the plan.

A work simplification expert, Alan Moganson, has made a career of introducing that concept to enterprises. He reportedly has worked in over 500 companies. One of these companies, Texas Instruments, credits 10 percent of its annual net profits to the beneficial suggestions from employees who have used work simplification techniques in discovering and developing improvements in work methods. I am convinced that plans like the Scanlon Plan and work simplification, which provide monetary incentives for helping to improve productivity, are the key to pay administration. Incentives that draw the best performance out of a group on a project are, in my judgment, better than incentives that reward solo performances. Special pay incentives for supervisors and managers in some form of bonuses should also be a part of any pay system.

RECRUITING PEOPLE TO FILL THE RANKS

I believe we could speed up our nation-building processes if every organization, both public and private, acted as if it were a microcosm of a foundation specializing in social and economic development. From this philosophy it logically follows that every organization should be deeply interested in environmental protection and the development of human resources through fair employment and effective staff development and utilization. It should encourage and assist the pre-entry education institutions, and it should encourage its employees to involve themselves in community development activities during their leisure time.

This outlook on community responsibility would require

good bridge building, and this in turn would facilitate recruitment. For example, if a company were to help the local community college plan curriculum and faculty needs and provide space and staff for some of its off-campus courses, it would have taken a positive recruitment step. There are many other ways to build linkages that aid in recruitment. Positive recruitment beats the practice of letting our employment office sit and wait for walk-ins to come asking for work. The walk-ins too often are unemployable.

Another lesson I have learned over the years about recruitment is that hand-to-mouth recruitment is poor economics and a real handicap in getting one's fair share of the best the labor market has to offer. Analysis of turnover data can tell any enterprise what its loss rate has been, by occupational category, over any specified period. Analysis of age data on today's staff can help the analyst adjust turnover projections for the retirement factor. By applying a safety factor to turnover data, one can project minimum recruitment needs and plan recruitment campaigns in coordination with seasonal supply and demand factors such as high school and college graduation dates.

Stockpiling a reasonable amount of high-potential manpower and feeding it into vacancies as they occur is better management than filling isolated vacancies one at a time after they have occurred and with individuals of only average or marginal qualifications. I assume that nearly every organization has ways of making productive use of talent for an interim period pending permanent assignment. Special projects, vacations, leave, illnesses, jury duty, military reserve duty, deaths, maternity, and committees and task forces all generate demand for ad hoc personnel. Interim duty can be a valuable part of the indoctrination of new employees, save the erosive effect of having a vacancy for weeks or months, and help upgrade the level of competency that comes from a more relaxed and intelligent recruitment approach.

There are many useful techniques of recruitment. Here are some that I have found especially helpful:

Search committees. These are select groups of individuals who have the background for conducting the recruitment and selection of persons best qualified for a particular position. It would be uneconomical to use this approach for filling every position, but it is well worth the investment in filling overall leadership and managerial posts. The committee needs an executive secretary to attend to the formalities and paperwork.

In-house advertising. I believe in advertising all vacancies through in-house media. Any other policy is destructive to morale and to confidence in top management.

Want ads. A well-worded want ad in selected newspapers and professional journals can be a rich source of candidates, especially for professional, scientific, and administrative positions. The responses should be directed to a post office box. The ad may attract several hundred responses, from which the search committee can select the best for further inquiry.

Employment agencies. These agencies are generally not good at finding qualified candidates for all types of work. They specialize. Some are known for their success in finding good material for executive positions. Others are better at highly professional jobs such as engineering specialists. Some cater to clerical job applicants. One should be precise in stating the qualification requirements to the agency and follow up regularly to keep its attention.

Brochure mailouts. An attractive and informative brochure mailed with good timing to educational institutions supplying people for work in a specialized field is a good technique. Student placement offices post such brochures on campus bulletin boards, and they will nearly always draw some response.

Recruitment teams. Two-person teams can be used very effectively for recruiting college students for professional, technical, and administrative work, provided the necessary advance planning is done. A personnel representative with full knowledge of pay, fringe benefits, and career opportunities should be on the team. The other member should be someone from the substantive field where new employees are needed.

Professional societies. These societies are good clearinghouses for job applicants and employers. Newsletters, society meetings, and society headquarters are all useful in getting interested parties together.

SELECTING THE BEST TALENT AVAILABLE

Systematic replenishment of manpower is essential to the continuity of goods and services from any organization. Everyone would agree that to consistently hire the first candidate for any job opening would be folly. Reliable methods of selection are therefore needed.

The goal, of course, is to select the best talent available—a goal not easily attained. Its attainment depends on a healthy balance between transfer and promotion from within and the selection of outsiders.

Interviewing is universally used as a basis for selection. Unfortunately, it is not reliable. Yet, countless jobs in countless organizations are being filled every year on the basis of a single interview.

There are some preliminary steps to good selection. Intelligent planning is a necessity. A sound set of valid qualification standards for the class of positions in which the vacancy falls, with graduated differences for each "grade" or level of responsibility in the class, is also required. One needs a clear, current description of the duties and responsibilities of the position to be filled. This is commonly called "position description" or "job description."

Furthermore, top management and all of us in personnel

administration need to be unwavering in our commitment to the equal opportunity concept. We must, in philosophy and practice, see to it that selection and advancement are based on ability, knowledge, and skills, under fair and open competition. This commitment also binds us to working to upgrade women and minorities without engaging in reverse discrimination practices; to treating "old Turks" and "young Turks" alike in selection (that is, age and seniority alone will not be made decisive factors); to avoiding the practice of nepotism, which can seriously undermine morale and interrupt control and communication; and to refrain from the practice of guaranteeing promotions in level of responsibility to individuals without regard to their total past performance.

Our philosophy on selection should also bind us to an active training, education, and development program for employees generally in order to afford all employees an opportunity to do their work in the most effective manner possible and to develop their fullest potential within the career field of their choice.

Selection is best when it is not hurried. With positive recruitment and the practice of stockpiling reserves for interim assignments and eventual placement to fill spots left by normal turnover, selection is made easier. Another advantage of interim assignments is that they conceptually serve the same purpose as the probationary appointment, with one difference: whereas the latter has never worked very well in practice, because supervisors seldom have the courage to terminate a probationary appointment, the former does work. If we in the personnel office could retain the option of determining performance during the interim period, we might have more success in making the final placement or terminating the individual from the payroll. The point is, in filling positions other than routine clerical or custodial jobs, find a way to see the candidate in action before he or she is set in concrete in a permanent position. Sometimes it can be done by detail (temporary job assignment), understudy assignment, internship, task force, or an acting capacity.

My experience indicates that multiple judgment is far superior to the single judgment in selection. This suggests selection methods such as selection panels, search committees, assessment centers, retreats, and progressive interviews by diversely interested persons—not just the supervisor and the supervisor's supervisor. It may mean interviews by prospective peers, people from other substantive but related fields, and even a prospective subordinate.

Reference checks on outside applicants are virtually worthless when they are done routinely over the telephone by a personnel clerk calling another personnel clerk. The personnel folder seldom contains any definitive data on conduct, performance, and potential. For professional, technical, scientific, managerial, and executive positions, I believe it would be well worth the investment to do more than call or write for vouchers on applicants. The prospective employer needs to make as much of a "full field" investigation on conduct, performance, and potential as it does in checking on the candidate's national loyalty and job suitability. The cost of an error in selection to fill jobs in these categories can be catastrophic, especially if the organization lacks the know-how and courage for weeding out incompetency.

DEALING WITH LABOR

Soundly conceived personnel administration, consistently applied, is the best prevention of and antidote for labor–management strife and its interruptions to the economy. I do not claim any expertise in the complicated legal and regulatory machinery it takes to deal with labor–management issues. There are plenty of authors who do have that expertise, and I will not attempt to paraphrase or duplicate their counsel. Permit me, however, to mention a few observations on the matter.

Incentives. A profit-sharing system is critical. I am convinced that employees of no organization will ever be very happy with a fixed share of the value of goods and services sold. They are not satisfied to see owners and top executives taking the profits and large salaries while they continue on fixed income with what they consider minimum adjustments for cost of living. They want a "piece of the action." Professional football is a striking analogy. The players negotiate for salaries and benefits. Beyond that they are interested in a share of the profits or bonuses from bowl games. Presumably, that motivates them to play harder to help produce a winning team. I am impressed with the Scanlon Plan as a good example of group rewards for increased productivity. M.I.T. has good resource material on this plan.

Training and development of supervisors and managers. This is another foundation of good relations between labor and management. Despite emphasis on the training of first- and second-level supervisors and middle managers since the World War I era, we still have not learned how to do it very well. The courses we use are bland and unimaginative in both substance and method. They range from 10 to about 60 hours in length and add up to too little too late. The supervisor's training needs begin *before* he takes charge of a work group, and his training needs continue indefinitely. Frill courses such as sensitivity training can be counterproductive.

Communication systems. Many organizations skimp as much on internal communication as they do on supervisor and manager training. The newspaper of my little home town died recently after over half a century of publication. The town will never be the same place again. There is no way for the local townspeople to announce new city services and objectives, record their progress, express their pride in individual and group achievements, officially note the loss of citizens, and the like. Residents will not have the same sense of belonging, and they will not be able to plan as intelligently. A group of people working together for a common employer have the same needs for communication as do the residents of a city.

Liaison. We need to have our personnel offices represented by individuals who are keen, informed, objective, and personable. It is not a role for a superannuated person who is coasting in to the finish line of his career or someone who is less than fully honest in his dealings. We need good listeners in the role, because union backing has often helped institute personnel measures that management itself should put forth on its own initiative. We are all aware of the subjects for bargaining, and it is not written in any labor–management agreement that only labor can initiate reforms in these subject areas. Likewise, we know what constitutes unfair labor practice, and it should be up to our liaison people to spot such practices and nip them in the bud.

Strike substitutes. Collective bargaining and the right to strike have to be protected in any free society. I believe we in personnel administration can greatly reduce the need for collective bargaining by better program planning. The chance of strikes will thus be lessened, and still further as we find new modes of settlement and new strike substitutes. Here are some current strike-substitute options:

- Non-stoppage strike—each side pays a penalty into a special fund, and leading citizens decide on the use of the money for worthy community purposes.
- Graduated strike—the union reduces the level of services until some minimum floor is reached that will not jeopardize welfare or safety. Pay for time not worked is lost in proportion to loss of service.

- Experimental negotiating agreement—involves a minimum guarantee plan, with the rest left to bargaining or arbitration. There is an advance agreement that there will be no strike.

We need to use these options more frequently and to develop a longer list of strike substitutes. It may well be true that labor is as uncomfortable with the strike weapon as management is. The mood of the public during crippling strikes and the soaring cost of living that often follows a settlement are barometers worth watching.

Legal counsel. Bargaining and arbitration are often reduced to a battle of wits between attorneys for both sides. Management's side of the issues should be presented by able, fair-minded persons who are well respected in their profession and the community at large. We damage our case with all concerned when we engage persons of marginal talent to use sharp practice as they represent us.

ADMINISTERING SPECIAL BENEFITS

Special benefits of the American worker are no longer an inconsequential or "fringe" element of compensation for services rendered. They can amount to a third or more of real income. As a trustee of the oldest and one of the largest prepaid group practice health maintenance organizations (HMOs) in the United States, I'm well aware of the scope and value of such benefits to a medical staff. During negotiations of a labor–management agreement in the spring of 1978, we agreed to a basic annual salary for physicians which brings those in specialty fields and with a few years of work experience in the HMO to some $80,000. However, we estimate that the effective annual income of these physicians before taxes is $120,000. The 31 special benefits are:

Free office space and utilities within a good work environment.
Equipment and supplies appropriate to specialty.
Support staff, including nurses, physicians' assistants, and appointment clerks.
Full range of laboratory services without charge.
Marketing staff to get new HMO members and replace turnover.
Administrative staff to collect from members, handle complaints, coordinate member relations services, and the like.
Health care (high option) for self and family.
Dental care for self and family. Spouse pays $1.00 monthly; children under 13 pay 50¢ per month and those age 13 to 22, $1 per month.
Continuation of health and welfare benefits during retirement.
Health and welfare benefits for dependents after physician is deceased.
Disability insurance.
Life insurance.
Workers' compensation.
Retirement at one-half the cost until 1/1/79, then at no cost.
Malpractice insurance without cost.
Education and career development benefits of five days per year at full pay.
Right to practice at local hospitals enough to retain hospital privilege.
Ten legal holidays annually.
Holiday on physician's birthday.
Twenty days of vacation leave in first eight years, and 25 days from then onward.
Fifteen days sick leave without limit on carryover from year to year.

Emergency leave of three days per year.
Administrative leave as required.
Excused absences with full pay in case of inclement weather.
Military leave, with differential payable as amount between HMO pay and military pay.
Sabbatical leave.
Jury and witness duty at differential pay equal to differential between jury or witness duty pay and HMO pay.
Dues for membership in three medical societies.
Licensing fees in several surrounding jurisdictions in which practice may be required by the HMO.
Free parking.
Three months' severance pay for nonprobationary physicians who may be separated involuntarily, except if dismissed for moral misconduct.

The above-listed benefits include only those with monetary rewards to the employee. There are others that may not affect pocketbook but which offer an intangible benefit for the employee. These include such things as organized recreational opportunities, credit union, convenience goods and services, emergency room and health care examination and counseling services, flexible work hours, and released time for work–study arrangements.

It is my experience that some employees derive more self-fulfillment from special benefits than they do from their basic take-home pay. Therefore, it behooves each of us in personnel administration to plan, organize, and administer each of these benefits with imagination, patience, and a genuine attitude of service. There are several propositions that strike me as being permanently useful generalizations about special benefits:

• Employees don't understand the benefit package. They regard the policies and procedures governing each benefit about the way many of us regard insurance policies—a legalistic document with a lot of fine print.

• The benefit package therefore needs interpreting. The intrinsic value of each benefit should be stated in real income terms repeatedly, as we communicate with the employee through his pay envelope, house organs, and other media.

• We should be alert for unusual benefits that fit the individual needs of employees at various stages of their career development and aging. For example, the option to purchase extra amounts of term insurance may be important at one stage but not at others. Perhaps employees need a *choice* among a longer list of benefits, with a cap on the aggregate real income value of benefits to be subsidized in whole or in part by the employer. There need be no limit on those benefits that employees are willing to buy for themselves.

In brief, we can make the benefit package a vehicle for a more rewarding work experience and a stimulant to two-way communication.

REWARDING THE HIGH PRODUCERS

The farmer could not have said it better than he did when he reportedly told the salesman with better-farming books, "Don't need your books, son—not farming as well now as I know how."

I was reminded of this wise saying recently while reading what one of my esteemed peers in personnel administration has to say on behavioral science. He is calling for more research money with which to do behavioral research. He is disturbed about the difference in amounts of money spent on the moon probe and on behavioral research. He wants to see more grants with which to study various aspects of productivity, industrial organization, and job satisfaction. He is encouraged to note that a recent grant will study the question of "how to engineer work for human effectiveness."

I have a different point of view on behavioral science research. Precious as the things discovered from behavioral science may be, I am aware of frightfully little discovered by behavioral science that mature people did not already know. The most famous of all behavioral science research projects, the Hawthorne plant (AT&T) experiment, found that people will work very hard for a management they perceive to be genuinely interested in their welfare. At the risk of heresy, I say this was not such a profound discovery.

We have known about rewards and penalties for a long time. My plea would therefore be that we reappropriate any grant money my friend the behavioral science advocate gets and use it to make some progress in certain fundamentals, such as:

- Intensify and refine the processes for selecting, training, and developing supervisors, middle managers, and executives—that is, improve leadership at all levels.
- Secure from every supervisor, manager, and executive a full commitment to search out the highest potential in all employees and to recognize their contributions in appropriate ways.
- Accelerate the use of the team approach to work, using the work-centered motivation concept.
- Emphasize *group* awards.
- Award the *real achievers* who have attained their objectives. Do not fall into the trap of allowing awards to be used as a political or manipulative in-house device to spur or reward the "brass" only.

Rewards and penalties are still the best way to go. Any employer that never fires a marginal producer is as mismanaged as one that never rewards a high achiever. It takes both. On the reward side of the coin, the best strategy I believe is a combination of realistic incentives and a system of group and individual rewards.

The 1948 GM-UAW agreement and the Scanlon Plan, both discussed earlier in this chapter, are landmark examples of good incentives systems. The first included a significant clause that held out the carrot of more pay for the "annual improvement factor" in productivity per employee man-hour. Scanlon's formula called for joint labor–management committees to gather employee suggestions on how to improve efficiency, reduce production costs, and eliminate waste, with gains from such efforts to be shared through steady employment, higher wages, and better working conditions. When plans like these are in place, social pressure from the group is brought to bear on individual members who may be inclined not to give a full measure of their talents and energies.

There is no shortage of ways in which to reward the real achievers. This, of course, should be an agenda item in continuing labor–management dialogs. Examples include cash bonuses, stock options, and increased subsidization of special benefits such as health insurance plans.

Individual rewards still have a place in my strategy for use of rewards and penalties. Recognition systems such as the Nobel, Pulitzer, and Motion Picture Academy prizes and awards are universally accepted in our culture. Basically, they go to individuals. Significantly, however, when the recipient receives such an award he or she typically acknowledges that the achievement would not have been possible without the combined efforts of Tom, Dick, and Harriet. In the tennis world, which I know from over 50 years of active participation, there are both group and individual awards. The Davis Cup goes annually to the winning national *team;* the Wimbledon trophy goes to the winning male singles player and to the winning female singles player. Olympic awards go to both national teams and individuals.

There are some reward systems that do not work so well when used as the single means of recognition. Cash awards for beneficial suggestions are an example. I have seen many suggestion box networks that were gathering dust. Another example is the use of letters and commendations. This is a cheap way out for any employer and reminds me of a dormitory newspaper which always bore the inscription in the masthead, "Costs nothing and worth it." Used in combination with more meaningful rewards, such as merit promotions, it can add the extra touch like the mint one finds at the exit of a good restaurant after a delicious meal.

HANDLING THE NON-PRODUCERS

If supervisors and managers were ever to have a situation where production and morale are consistently high, they would cease to earn their pay. They are in place essentially to do for *people* what good mechanics do for equipment—preventive maintenance and troubleshooting. They also cease to earn their pay when they begin to neglect either of these phases of the work. The easiest to neglect is the troubleshooting part, because it can backfire and cause very uncomfortable repercussions.

"Preventive maintenance" in people work consists of all the positive things the supervisor or manager does to train, encourage, and utilize the knowledge, skills, and abilities of the individual. There is no substitute for such measures as proper placement, pay commensurate with responsibility, recognition and rewards, and mutual assistance in developing the individual's potential for making meaningful contributions to the enterprise and realizing a fulfilling career in doing so. Good supervision should establish the foundations for good relations by (1) letting each worker know how he or she is getting along, (2) giving credit when due, (3) telling employees in advance about changes that will affect them, and (4) making the best use of each person's ability.

Non-production in a work unit is almost a surefire barometer report that the system of personnel administration is not functioning properly in an organization. If it is working as it should, the situation will not persist very long. Remedial measures will be taken. As in the case of a good school system, where a child's performance is found to be below his performance capabilities, the cause is identified. It may be reading, hearing, or seeing difficulties. Remedial steps are taken to correct the root cause.

An indispensable element in handling non-production is a well-conceived and meticulously kept system of personnel files. Few organizations realize this, I am afraid, or if they do, they often fall down in following through. Their files are frequently bare when it comes time to take some action. What would the medical people do without clinical records? What would maintenance people do without maintenance records?

One of the problems is that we personnel people have insisted on a single, centrally kept personnel file on each employee. For this to work presupposes that operating people provide continuous and up-to-date reports for the file, since nearly all the action about an employee takes place at the work scene, not in the personnel office. But operating people lack the time and inclination to write formal memoranda to record the bright and dark sides of an employee's performance and conduct. They can do it with handwritten notes scribbled on assorted bits and pieces of paper, and probably would if they were encouraged to do so.

Therefore, the first step is to have a meeting of minds on how the record system is to work and who is to work it. Unless you can solve that problem, you might as well forget your chances of dealing sucessfully with non-production.

Now comes the troubleshooting part of personnel work. With a personnel *presence* in operations, as suggested above, instances of non-production can easily be spotted. Once a supervisor has had a successful experience in having you help in dealing with non-production, your business will be continuous. Supervisors communicate among themselves and the news of your usefulness will spread.

As you accept your "first case," you will start by doing the necessary reconnaissance to get the facts, then weigh and decide on a course of action. You may discover that it is merely a personality conflict and a reassignment is in order. Or you may discover that external factors are temporarily affecting performance. Hopefully, you will find an administrative officer centrally in the department or branch where the problem exists. Administrative officers can provide extremely valuable assistance in coordinating action and gathering other perspectives on the situation. They can guide you to the other interested parties—the union, legal counsel, upper echelons of management, and others—as the case progresses.

Above all, you must make a commitment to yourself to persevere until the case has been thoroughly investigated and you have rendered the wisest and most objective conclusion and recommendation you are capable of rendering.

Depending on the facts you turn up and the conclusion you reach from your own analysis and consultation with others, you have a series of options to consider in making your recommendation. Remember that you are obliged to exhaust administrative remedies before undertaking more drastic action. These are illustrative:

Reengineer the job. Mary Parker Follett wrote brilliantly on this subject in the late 19th century.*

Retrain the individual to make his skill capabilities more nearly match the job requirements.

* *Dynamic Administration.* The Collected Papers of Mary Parker Follet. Edited by Henry C. Metcalf and L. Urwick. New York and London: Management Publications Trust, 1941. 320 pages.

Generate peer pressures to equalize production among individuals doing similar work.
Counsel.
Reassign the individual.
Issue a letter of warning and make progress checks on performance.
Suspend from duty without pay.
Prepare to take an adverse action. Prefer charges, in writing, with a specified deadline for reply.

In this connection, I believe large organizations would do well to install a system of hearings similar to the circuit court system of justice in the United States. We have to find some way to cut down on the paperwork involved in adverse action cases. This nearly always places supervisors and managers on the defensive and discourages them from taking the initiative in adverse action cases. Consequently, non-production cases stagnate and have the same ever-widening effect that a bad apple has in a whole barrel of apples. Another analogy is the small claims court system, which tends to streamline and simplify the process of giving a hearing to both parties without going through all the formalities of a regular court case proceeding.

If the adverse action involves removal or downgrading of an individual, the personnel office must not drop out of the case when the action has been sustained. It has a responsibility to follow through with all of the compassionate and constructive help it is capable of giving. Outplacement services may be needed. It is necessary to check on the impact the action had on production. Finally, it is critical that the organization learns something from the non-production-handling experience and that that lesson be entered in the organization's permanent memory system for future reference. Thus, the loop is completed.

SEEING PEOPLE OFF TO OTHER OPPORTUNITIES

A loss from the ranks of any enterprise is of serious consequence, regardless of the cause. Sudden death, dismissal for cause, resignation because of dissatisfaction, transfer to a better job, reductions in force, and promotion to a higher level of responsibility within the same organization are but some of the reasons why individuals are lost to a particular work unit.

Such losses inevitably drain off valuable experience that is costly to restore. They may also cause the spread of a feeling that the departed employees were unfairly treated or exploited. Obviously, therefore, losses can impact on recruitment, training and development, employee relations, public relations, productivity and morale, and the cost of doing business.

We personnel people are not dealing with losses very intelligently. Occasionally, we are stirred to launch another attack on the problem of turnover, often by reinstating the old exit interview process. This accomplishes little or nothing, for people leaving with grievances simply do not level with exit interviewers. They know that disclosure of their true feelings could haunt them in future job opportunities. So they clam up and give "personal reasons" as the basis for leaving. We callously regard turnover as an inevitable condition, failing to sense that one loss may foretell a string of losses, a downturn in productivity, and dramatic rises in costs. We tend not to go near the scene where the loss originated to smoke out the real reasons.

One of the most serious areas of neglect in the loss picture is that of the older worker. Some managers "wage war" against older workers who show no signs of being willing to close shop and take their retirement. Discriminatory practices became so rampant that the Congress of the United States in 1978 enacted legislation to relax mandatory retirement age limits. My best guess is that this will in no way inhibit those managers who believe that once an individual reaches a certain chronological age, he or she is "over the hill" and deserving of nothing better than a shove in the direction of the EXIT sign. And we personnel people have too often looked the other way as these discriminatory practices occurred. It is an area where our counseling and utilization services should be concentrated.

The last official action we take on an employee should be the most efficiently processed of all. The manner in which that action is handled (or mishandled) will go with the employee and reside in his mind for years to come. Some personal touch should be added to the action document on which the separation is formally described.

Outplacement services can pay tremendous dividends. I knew an individual who uprooted himself in a distant state and moved himself and family to an East Coast city to begin life anew, only to receive, after three months on the job, a reduction-in-force notice due to the failure of anticipated funding to materialize. Over 300 other employees were similarly affected. The organization salvaged its image by arranging to have interviewers from a number of other organizations on the premises as soon as the notices of termination went out. Practically all terminated employees were offered jobs at equal or better pay.

Another area of serious neglect concerns people who retire after working a lifetime in an organization. We personnel people fail to perceive that these are, and will continue to be, major "stockholders" in the enterprise. They can run the value of our enterprise's goodwill account up or down by the way they treat us in talking and acting on the outside and in their continuing relations with their contacts within our labor force. It would cost so little to keep them on the mailing list of the house organ and to see that they get special invitations to special events such as the annual picnic or the dedication of a new plant. The point is that we ought not to neglect to follow through on the goal of keeping influential oldtimers safely within the embrace of our "extended family."

SHARING INFORMATION WITH EMPLOYEES

We personnel specialists have traditionally cited orientation as an essential element of sound personnel administration. And we have consistently done orientation poorly. We tend to do it on the entrance upon duty date, in a fixed amount of time (often only an hour or two), and without the use of multimedia instruction. Our concept of orientation fails to recognize the absolute necessity for *continuing* orientation of the employee and for the involvement of non-personnel office participants in the process.

Orientation should begin during the pre-employment phase of the new relationship. The first-level supervisor or foreman should pick up where the personnel office leaves off with its formal orientation. The personnel office can continue the orientation through in-house news organs, a loose-leaf or pamphlet series system of informational materials, audiovisual media and self-instructional material, bulletin boards, special notices in the organization's formal issuance system, and the like.

I have consistently had success with a system of indoctrination through what I call the "vestibule" system of entry. Instead of marching the new employee (particularly the clerical or secretarial employee) off to his or her permanent assignment, assign the individual to a work place under the jurisdiction of the training and development group. A master craftsperson is in charge. The unit takes in real work projects from operating groups and gets out the work with employees who are temporarily on assignment there. They are released as soon as they individually reach a satisfactory level of proficiency and learn the modus operandi of the enterprise under the wing of someone who not only knows the policies and procedures thoroughly but is also a master teacher. Such a person, of course, encourages the new employee and more nearly ensures complete success on the permanent assignment.

The vestibule system and the "buddy" system are far from being comparable. Buddies perpetuate ineffective work practices and negative attitudes. Quality control in the vestibule system is maintained through the selection of the vestibule supervisor.

The library should also be enlisted in the continuing orientation effort. Modern libraries have great potential as continuing information centers. For example, they can selectively route professional and scientific literature to individuals who are focusing on a particular subject in their work. Their capability for retrieving and synthesizing material on related parts of a subject is unmatched elsewhere in the organization.

Finally, I would commend the concepts of participative management and multiple management as effective means of internal communication. When employees are encouraged to assist in the decision-making process, it sets them in motion to gather factual data with which to weigh and decide the issues. Information they search out on their own initiative may well be more meaningful than information they did not reach for.

SUPPORTING EMPLOYEE GROWTH AND DEVELOPMENT

It is my considered judgment that the function of employee training, education, and development does not belong in the personnel department. The rationale for this position has already been stated in this book. Nevertheless, this proposition does not completely relieve us in the personnel office of responsibility in this area. I see certain residual responsibilities:

- We need to set the tone in our recruitment efforts, indicating that our employer is fully responsible and committed to a program of continuing training, education, and development of its staff.
- In our operation of counseling services, we need counselors who are skilled in identifying cases where training and development are apparently at the core of the problem. And we have to have counselors who refer cases in which they are lacking the necessary competency to solve the problem.
- We can stimulate managers and supervisors to be more active in the identification of employees with growth potential as we carry on our placement and utilization functions.
- We can identify individuals in the work force who have the talents and motivation to become "people developers." They may perform this function as an integral part of their operating responsibilities or as members of the training and development staff.
- We can collaborate with the training and development staff and make constructive suggestions for areas of need, new curriculum, and priorities.
- In the referral of eligible candidates for promotional opportunities, we can reward employees who make the most of training and development experiences and distinguish themselves as high achievers.
- We can trace the growth and development of individual employees through good records management.
- We can assemble human resources rosters of talent, composed of retired employees and current employees available for part-time and overtime duty, to bid against the outside market on projects of an urgent nature.
- We can draw on the services of the training and de-

velopment staff to help make upward mobility and equal opportunity a reality by upgrading the skills of individuals.

- We can negotiate work–study plans with cooperative education institutions and encourage the inflow of research fellows, interns, and apprentices.
- We can negotiate and monitor training and promotion agreements under which operating officials carefully select and intensively develop professional, scientific, and managerial candidates for positions at the jouneyman level.

Chapter 6

Stage Three: Assuring Growth and Development of the Personnel Staff

Of all the staffs in an organization, the personnel department staff seems the logical choice for demonstrating what an investment in human resources can achieve. The personnel staff has as its ultimate mission the maximum effective selection, placement, and utilization of each and every employee in its parent organization. It must therefore live as a shining example of human resources development if it is to retain its prerogative of admonishing operating departments and other staff groups to do better by their human resources.

There are a number of in-house and outside methods which any personnel department dedicated to this cause can use in managing the continuing growth and development of its own staff. They are described in this chapter.

IN-HOUSE POSSIBILITIES

Conferences. In a democratic society, meetings and conferences are constantly being held in all organizations for planning and operational purposes. Some are ad hoc; others recur on a predictable cycle. Some have as their objective the systematic review of the status of operations; others aim to apply multiple judgment to such issues as the allocation of resources, development of staff, pay and fringe benefits, new services, systems, and operational strategies.

The personnel staff can gain in countless ways from active participation in selected conferences, and even from monitoring them as observers. The presence of selected personnel staff members in conferences conducted by operations officers builds a more effective liaison between the personnel office and its clients, because the personnel official can stay better informed on program developments. To the extent that the personnel members actively participate, their input into the conference means preparation, deeper thinking, and some mind-stretching. Communication skills are sharpened.

The personnel members' contacts are broadened as their awareness of who's who in operations is increased. They gain additional name recognition and perhaps improve their image and stature. Relationships formed in conferences can be lasting relationships from which the employer can long benefit. Operators and personnel people alike may get some answers to questions about which they have long thought and held some preconceived biases.

A conference that is well conceived and managed can be a rich experience for participants. It helps restore their perspective, their incentive to explore new directions, and their energy reserves. Such conferences are, in my judgment, very cost-effective from a time investment standpoint. Whoever said the camel is the product of a committee (conference) that set out to build a horse was a cynic and a fool.

In-house training and development activities. Progressive organizations have a liberal offering of these. They go by such names as courses, seminars, workshops, institutes, and symposia. Three things can be gained or improved by these activities: knowledge, skills, and attitudes. For example, a wage and compensation officer could increase his knowledge of economics; an employment specialist could improve her skill in job analysis; and an employee relations counselor could broaden his understanding of the housing, employment, and upward mobility needs of low- to medium-income persons who were underprivileged during their pre-adult years.

Personnel officials and technicians cannot and need not actively participate in all in-service training activities. They should be selective and in some cases merely monitor a particular program in whole or in part. They may be asked to develop a component and to teach it—a fine development experience in itself. Attendance regardless of status as a participant can keep the personnel person better oriented with respect to programmatic developments, policies and regulations, systems and procedures, and organizational adjustments. This awareness is vital.

Use of in-house training and development programs as a staff development experience has many incidental benefits. It affords one the opportunity to establish direct relationships with individuals in other branches of the organization, and these relationships are usually superior to telephone or memorandum relationships. In other words, communication is facilitated. Besides filling the specific need to know, participation in in-house training and development activities can demonstrate one's commitment to continued professional growth. In some organizations, in-house activities of this nature are part on-the-clock and part off-the-clock and therefore are a measure of one's own interest in and commitment to self-development.

Incident process. This is an offshoot of the case study method of teaching. The instructor describes or presents a written statement of a critical incident as it occurred and asks participants to resolve the matter in a manner that will restore productivity and harmonious relations. Fact sheets are distributed as key questions are asked by participants. Options for dealing with the incident emerge and each participant clusters about the one of his choice. Advocates of each option caucus and their spokesperson presents the rationale for action. The instructor or resource person then smokes out the major issues, critiques each option, and comments on such established principles and processes of modern management as the incident may help to identify.

Since much personnel work of necessity pertains to incidents with impact on productivity and labor–management relations, this method is very applicable. It is good practice in decision making through an orderly process of fact finding, analysis, weighing and deciding among options, and presenting solutions convincingly. It enables one to practice communication skills such as conference leadership and the give and take of constructive debate. The coordinator role is usually rotated as each new incident is introduced. This process stimulates reflective thinking as the details of an incident continue to weigh on the participant's mind long after the session ends. One of the most significant benefits of the interaction and peer pressure is the effect it seems to have on members who tend to decide human relations issues in an authoritarian style.

Essentially, this method of learning is based on realism rather than theory. Any organization using this method for staff development can, after the use of a few professionally developed materials on real incidents, develop a series grounded in its own operations and expand this "band" as each new group has its turn at coping with a series of incidents.

Programmed instruction. This method of instruction grew from the research and teachings of Professor B. F. Skinner of Harvard several decades ago. Increasingly, this and other forms of individualized instruction are finding acceptance in both industry and government. Educators have long recognized individual differences in learners, but they lacked the technology and the staff to cope with the learning problems on an individual basis. Group instruction therefore became the prevailing mode, and the tendency too frequently has been to work with an excessively large teacher–student ratio.

Programmed instruction (PI) is learner-paced. The learner can go as rapidly or as slowly as he or she comfortably can. The material is broken into bits and pieces, called frames, and presented in logical sequences. The learner is tested frequently, and, to reinforce learning, is required to repeat sequences in which mistakes were made.

There are many advantages of this form of instruction for the personnel staff. It is cheaper. Learning can take place at the office or even at home. Travel costs are eliminated. Scheduling of the training can be done between workload peaks. The classroom instructor is eliminated. There is a lower capital investment in curriculum development (provided the material is already in a PI repository—and this repository is expanding rapidly). Faster start-ups can be made when commercially available PI material is obtainable.

The PI method can be modified to fit particular situations. Periodically, a resource person can be brought to the group taking a given PI course to answer questions and help with difficult problems. The PI method can be used with or without teaching machines. Computer-assisted instruction (CAI) is a form of PI that opens a vast field of input and output machine technology.

The Industrial College of the Armed Forces, Washington,

D.C., has trained thousands of military personnel and civilians worldwide by the oldest form of PI known—correspondence courses. Typically, the education and experience levels of its participants are comparable to those of professional personnel staffs. The use of audiovisual aids in most PI training raises the PI method well above traditional correspondence course design. I am therefore enthusiastic about this possibility for the continuing development of personnel staffs.

Retreats. Personnel offices can be like busy fire stations. The workers are so busy fighting "fires" that they have no time to think about fire prevention or the repair and improvement of their methods, equipment, and tools. The concept of a retreat is just right for personnel people. Someplace about 100 miles away from the usual place of business offers relative freedom from distraction and an opportunity to think more deeply about their work.

A well-planned retreat can bring some self-renewal in spirit and physical energies. By inviting resource people to the retreat, there can be some exposure to contemporary thought—some mind-stretching. It is also an opportunity to get to know and interact with peers in other specialized fields of personnel management, which should be the goal of all good personnel departments. Having a few senior executives of the company or public agency present for selected portions of the retreat affords an opportunity to present ideas to policymakers in an atmosphere that may be more conducive to reasoned judgment.

Retreats should focus on the larger issues and options for solving human resources problems. Issues considered should pertain to such matters as employment policy, recruitment strategies, utilization practices, labor–management relations, compensation policy, position classification practice, incentives, and performance evaluation.

Retreats can improve communication with the staff, strengthen morale, and chart common goals for the future.

Management games. Perhaps the most effective of all training methods for a personnel staff is one in which simulation or experiential techniques are used. Role playing, for example, has long been used successfully in human relations training. In a real sense, the management game is role playing. To be sure, some management games require the use of very sophisticated equipment, such as the computer. The Link Trainer was introduced years ago as a means of simulating flight for pilot trainees, and simulation devices are commonly used now in training high school students how to drive an automobile safely before they are ever authorized to get behind the wheel of a real car on the road.

There are many advantages to management games for personnel staff, and it is my judgment that this method should be used much more in the future. It greatly reduces the risk factor and the cost of an error. It offers the staff an opportunity for creativity in contributing to the scenarios of the game. It is a fast, intensive way to build experience. It can demonstrate the value of integrated personnel management and the superiority of team effort over solo practice. The game atmosphere ensures undivided attention and incites a competitive spirit, which can bring out the best in the players. Like the retreat, it takes the staff away from the distractions of their offices and helps them focus on the larger issues of the organization.

Job rotation. It is difficult to see how a bank teller could ever learn banking on the teller window, or how the retail store clerk could ever learn merchandising on the cash register at the novelty counter. By the same token, a position classifier or any other personnel technician will never master the broader view of personnel management by being held indefinitely in his narrow specialty. "The grooves of specialization are ever deepening," said a favorite professor of mine, Dr. Cathryn Seckler-Hudson, over 30 years ago. The solution is job rotation. The medical profession learned this lesson generations ago. Our military services and foreign service and many of the most successful companies in the United States have regularly practiced job rotation for years. We know from management intern programs that job rotation is an aid to the ultimate placement and maximum utilization of the individual, because multiple judgment in the evaluation process is superior to the single judgment of any one supervisor.

Use of this principle can contribute to upward mobility and promotion-from-within objectives, thus lessening the need for bringing in outsiders, who can upset morale and productivity. New challenges from job rotation tend to restart the mind of the person who has become complacent in the routines of his job.

Another important result of job rotation is that the executive development process is furthered. It contributes to a growing reservoir of talent with a more broadly based experience than the narrow specialist has. Internal communication is facilitated. Persistent problems get a fresh push.

Professional societies. Some organizations seem to hold a provincial view of professional societies, discouraging their professional personnel from participating in such groups. Nothing could be poorer economics. Active participation in relevant professional societies should begin for junior personnel technicians as they are launched in their work, and such involvement should continue into the senior personnel executive ranks.

Professional societies represent an "off-limits" gathering place for people of common professional interests, where they can grow and contribute to the growth of others. The interchange of ideas, the feeling of security that comes from associating with others in like work, a forum for the expression of contemporary thought, a network to use in calling for information and advice on problems not previously encountered—these are but a few of the advantages.

Professional societies generate good materials, such as bibliographies, topic discussion papers, how-to pamphlets, and journals to which members can contribute manuscripts for possible publication. Their luncheon and dinner meetings attract distinguished guest speakers from a wide spectrum of social, economic, and political affairs. They can be a fountain of reforms that are needed in the professional field. In brief, they represent a continuing-education opportunity for the personnel staff at minimum cost.

Organizations should be willing to subsidize a share of the costs of membership and ongoing activities of at least one relevant professional society for each staff member. However, the individual's degree of active participation and his contributions to his society's work should be evaluated along with his on-the-job performance.

OUTSIDE POSSIBILITIES

Fairs and Exhibits. Some readers may recall the excitement that family farm members felt years ago when the annual state agricultural fair was held. Such families, before the days of radio, television, and improved highways, had a fairly isolated existence. There were prizes and a feast for the mouth and eyes of every member who was fortunate enough to make the trip to the big fair. Agriculture was advancing by leaps and bounds. Land grant colleges were generating the know-how, and perhaps the fairs were helping to fire the incentive of farmers and future farmers to excel.

Personnel people could well afford to emulate the agricultural fairs of states and counties. The award of significant prizes should be a part of the exercise. Fairs are such an efficient way to keep abreast of technology and contemporary thought. They dispense ideas. They provide incentive to reinforce trends, build new professional relationships, and replenish the feeling of pride one needs in one's professional field in order to give his best efforts.

Like several of the other methods suggested above, fairs and exhibits provide a cost-effective learning opportunity because they are intensive. Evidence collected at fairs and exhibits can be useful in the presentation of new goals, objectives, and program proposals to the chief executive officer of an organization.

Teaching assignments. It is commonly understood that the best way to learn a subject thoroughly is to have to teach it. Preparation requires a full measure of self-discipline and reflective thinking, research, writing skills, and an understanding of the multimedia approach to teaching. The teaching phase makes even heavier demands and is often very fatiguing, both mentally and physically.

Many advantages can flow from a teaching assignment well done. It can have a positive impact on conceptual planning, management practices, and organizational patterns. It can point up the need for higher standards of supervision and management, and for improved leadership at upper levels.

It is not uncommon for teaching assignments to aid in the identification of individuals with high potential who may be underemployed or underutilized. The person doing the teaching may, as a result of his or her performance, gain new stature and be recognized as a logical candidate for work of greater responsibility. This person is, of course, in an excellent position to spot participants whose assignment should be reexamined.

Teaching assignments can be inside or on the outside as an extracurricular activity. In either case, they can be a growth experience and they can generate a variety of by-products for wider dissemination, such as A/V aids, handouts, textual material, outlines, and bibliographies.

Community development. One of the finest laboratories in which a personnel worker can practice his trade is the community in which he or she lives. Leadership roles are always vacant, or the individual can enter the ranks of community developers at any desired level simply by volunteering for duty. The rewards at times may be even more self-fulfilling than one's bread-and-butter job. The impact on the social, economic, and political conditions in the community may make a real difference in its becoming a more desirable place in which to live.

The range of project possibilities is diverse. It includes schools, churches, recreation, youth, libraries, environment, safety, planning, political action, consumerism, service clubs, civic associations, League of Women Voters, and countless others. Taking an active role in the community activities of one's choice carries much less risk than similar involvement would at work, and thus enables one to take a bolder stance and to try new approaches to human relations and management improvement problems. It can be broadening and helpful in overcoming inhibitions. It can build confidence in verbal skills and in the art of organizing and managing work that has to be accomplished primarily through others.

The community role lets an employee practice good citizenship, and it contributes to keeping local government in responsible hands. The fallout effect on other family members, particularly children, can create a positive learning environment by example.

In brief, it seems to me to be good business for any organization to encourage its personnel staff to continue its growth and development by becoming actively involved in community development activities. It can redound to the organization's advantage in many ways.

Academic courses. It is a prime thesis of this book that organizations can and should divert subject matter specialists who have certain other competencies to key positions in the personnel management department. It follows, in my judgment, that these staff members should be encouraged to maintain currency in their substantive fields; further, in learning more about human resources development and personnel management, it may be to their advantage to take selected courses in outside educational institutions.

The mental discipline, the self-esteem gained from academic achievement, and the exposure to new and deeper thought all contribute to a sense of well-being. Further, this academic participation enables the individual and his organization to plow back into the business community some practical experience that should be beneficial. Sending only juniors to the academic world and never some able, more seasoned staff is not the way to influence the direction of thinking in the business community.

An organization that views the academic world as a place in which to do a part of its staff development is being a responsible member of the business community. The representatives it sends to the academic community should be asked to evaluate the experience as a basis for future outside course authorizations and for making suggestions to the institution's administrators.

Sabbatical leave. This means of staff development is commonly perceived as an experience primarily intended for the academic world. Relatively few employers make use of the method, which I believe has tremendous possibility. It should not be viewed as an earned excuse to take a prolonged vacation from work with full or partial pay. Surely, it can be an opportunity for thorough self-renewal through the replenishment of physical and mental energies. But there is more to it than that.

The sabbatical has all the latent possibilities that a scientific experiment has. The experience encompasses analysis of needs, project design, the operational phase, post-sabbatical critiques, and reportorial responsibilities. It may involve research, teaching, writing, travel, practical observation, experimental work, advanced academic studies, and the like.

This development method affords people time for meditation and reflection on their total past performance. There are family ramifications, too. I have noticed recently a significant number of younger, highly charged-up executives withdrawing from their political or executive roles with the statement that they needed to take time off to renew their acquaintance with spouse and children. The steady grind was to be replaced, they said, by a less regimented schedule and more leisure time.

Another advantage of this approach is that it can have a domino effect by permitting some temporary reassignments of other staff members. Hence, the multiplier effect is gained through job rotation. Since the employer is making a substantial investment, sabbaticals should be approved only for individuals who present and defend well-conceived and relevant project proposals. While it may be a mandatory requirement under a labor–management contract to award sabbaticals to selected classes of personnel after a specified number of years of service, the employer generally has the right to review and approve the project proposal and to require a post-sabbatical report. These options should be exercised intelligently.

Internships in small business. The catastrophic rate of failure among small business firms may well be related to the fact that they cannot afford a personnel office. The proprietor and, depending on the nature of the business, his or her whole family reportedly have to work long hours (12 or more per day) to make ends meet. In about 80 percent of the cases, according to the U.S. Department of Commerce, the family effort results in a business failure. A business failure usually means loss of assets, impairment of credit, wreckage of self-esteem, and other less tangible woes. Even the health of a principal may be undermined or destroyed.

One of the known causes of small business failure is lack of management expertise. To me, that suggests the absence in the small business of certain management specialists we take for granted in large business and public enterprises—for example, the personnel specialist, the training and development specialist, and the management analyst. The need for the skills of capable individuals in these disciplines begins when the entrepreneur adds the first employee, not the 100th or the 1,000th.

We use the services of a man who has made a lifetime career out of plumbing and electrical services, operating out of his private residence. His wife takes the incoming calls for service during the daytime, and he calls back in the evening to determine more specifically the nature of the problem. The man is extremely reliable, competent, and personable. His charges are moderate. The need for such craftsmen in the community is great. Therefore, when he came to our house recently to solve some problems I suggested that he should expand the size of his business and serve more people. Then he told me of his failure upon having tried just that.

There was a time, he said, when he had five craftsmen working for him, but at the end of the day he was a nervous wreck. All he did, he said, was follow around behind his subordinates and fix their mistakes—careless mistakes. He loves his work because he finds every problem different as he progresses through his day; plumbing and electrical problems require a good measure of innovation and creativity. He is a natural client for my mini-consulting service idea, for it is clear to me that he needed the part-time services of some management specialists as well as the full-time services of some plumbers and electricians to make his small business yield for him the same sense of self-fulfillment he continues to get from his solo practice. I wonder if he does not envy his peers who have branched out and expanded in other parts of the metropolitan area.

It seems to me that there is a place in the private sector for a sprinkling of mini-consulting firms which could, for a modest fee, provide an on-call service to the small business entrepreneur with about 100 or fewer employees. The helping firm would provide the basic management services including the systems work, work simplification, job design, recruitment and screening of job applicants, and skills training.

Therein lies, I believe, the opportunity for young people who represent the potential for a corps of future personnel specialists to get their basic training and experience. It could be to the business world what the Peace Corps, VISTA, and other human resources development programs have been to individuals who are interested in community development. Our military services have served a similar purpose for many young people who, upon graduation from high schoool, were not certain of the direction their career should take.

International assignments. Our economy is now tightly interlocked with the economies of other nations, rich and poor, large and small. The United States government has been engaged in bilateral foreign aid on a substantial scale since World War II—in some years with as many as 80 less developed countries. This has involved capital grants and technical assistance. Additionally, we help fund a number of international organizations that provide multilateral assistance for social and economic development. These organizations include the United Nations, the World Bank, the International Monetary Fund, and others.

In all these relationships, there is a continuous need for

Americans to fill positions at home and abroad to help in the planning, oversight, and evaluation of projects in which U.S. taxpayer monies are committed. As a nation, we do a frightfully poor job in preparing people for these international assignments. Granted that we have a few good colleges and universities that prepare people for foreign service officer positions of the State Department, what are we doing to fill the pipeline with competent individuals who have the aptitude and abilities for cross-cultural work in non-State Department public agencies and the entire private sector?

Having lived and worked overseas in a developing country, I have seen this need first-hand. It is real. Future personnel specialists in both our public and private sectors would gain immeasurably from overseas assignments in the formative stages of their careers, regardless of whether they ultimately settle into personnel specialist roles or in line operations or other staff specialties. It should almost be mandatory that a specialist working in employment and utilization or in employee training and development, in a public agency or private firm, have some resident overseas experience. A personnel specialist without a practical understanding of cross-cultural work has a tunnel-like vision.

Credentialing. One authority on personnel administration bemoans "overcredentialing in our society." I have just the opposite feeling about personnel administration; namely, that it is woefully *undercredentialed*.

Personnel specialists are insulted when anyone insinuates that theirs is not a line of *professional* work. Let's look at such work in perspective and see if by chance there is a double standard.

We expect our physicians to have undergone a rigorous, exhaustive course of study and internship totaling a dozen years or more before they are allowed to practice medicine. They pass a Medical Board examination administered in the state where they wish to practice, and they are licensed.

Take the certified public accountant. He studies accounting for years and climaxes his preparation by taking an intricate, comprehensive CPA examination administered by the state in which he wishes to practice accounting. The attorney is not someone who hangs out a shingle after a cursory reading of a few law book cases or after taking a few courses. He goes to law school for years, takes the Bar examination administered by the state where he proposes to practice law, passes or fails, and, if he passes, hangs out his shingle and starts his law practice.

Americans understand licensing, they accept it as a quality control, and they are prepared to deal rather harshly with any individual found operating without a proper license. The plumber, the barber, the electrician, the truck driver, the school teacher, the nurse, the airplane pilot, the architect, the speech therapist, the dentist, and countless other people in our society are licensed for the work they do. The license is based on a review of their qualifications and often on a performance test. Some are licensed only after a long apprenticeship involving both theory and practice.

Would you take your cat to a veterinarian who is unlicensed? Now stop reading for a few minutes, put this book aside, and confer with yourself about whether or not it is a good idea to continue to leave the personnel people free to practice without a license—on you or your cat.

Admittedly, it is not your or your cat's life at stake. Or is it? Your employment opportunities, the determination of your pay for the work you do, the promotional opportunities you can expect (or not expect) to come your way from meritorious performance, your working conditions, your protection against arbitrary and capricious actions, the quality of supervision you receive, and fringe benefits—all these make life more rewarding and ensure your ability to live out your life with dignity and self-respect. They vitally affect your state of mind, and a bad state of mind can undermine your health.

Are you willing to leave the responsibility for all of these "professional services" to a group, many of whose members have drifted into personnel work without a license, with no special training, and apparently with a negative attitude toward their responsibilities? Many individuals in personnel departments have openly admitted that they are working there because it offers them a better chance to brighten their own future. They are often the first to know about new programs and vacancies in ongoing programs, so they can be the first in line for such opportunities.

Much of the problem stems from the fact that there are no established sources of supply originating at the grass roots of our society to generate a corps of able personnel specialists. Have you ever heard of any family encouraging their children at an early age (or any age) to consider personnel administration as a life's work? You know, of course, that many families do press their young into channels that can lead to careers in law, medicine, engineering, journalism, dramatics, music, education, and countless other professional fields. Have you ever heard of a high school counselor guiding a young person into study of personnel administration? Do you know of any colleges or universities with a whole department or school devoted to personnel administration? I feel sure you do not.

This is not true of many presumably lesser fields. One of the hamburger chains now has a whole "university" for producing experts to run their hamburger outlets. Barber colleges are not uncommon. There are still some good secretarial schools to be found. Companies like Xerox have established multimillion-dollar training and development centers to train sales people, repair technicians, and managers. We have hotel management schools and cosmetology schools. Continuing education wings of major universities are working long hours to meet demands for basic and advanced knowledge in countless occupational fields. But you will find a very spotty offering of courses here and there to prepare people for the vital work of shaping the career direction, working conditions, and future of people from the earliest age at which they can legally work until they retire.

Something is very strange about the phenomenon of there being no known source of the members of the personnel administration "profession" and no licensing provisions. The existence of personnel departments is almost as mysterious as the phantom unidentified flying objects (UFOs). The difference is that some of us have never seen a UFO but we have all seen personnel departments, even though we don't know where their members came from. It is time, I believe, to legitimize personnel administration through credentialing and a national effort to establish a network of "generator" institutions with appropriate curricula and work–study arrangements functioning on both the domestic and international scenes.

Chapter 7

How to Get Started and Chart Your Progress

In a sense, this book advocates that those of us who now occupy senior-level positions in personnel departments and branch offices should abdicate. Under the British system of government, we would call for a vote of confidence and honorably abide by the outcome. Some of us perhaps would be retained, and others would be sent packing.

This could be the best thing that ever happened to all of us in personnel administration, regardless of our individual dispositions. As in the case of the Proposition 13 tax revolt in California in 1978, which soon spread to many other states and localities, some will consider the move to reform personnel administration nonsense and some will applaud wildly; but without exception, all will do some deep and reflective thinking on the matter. And, as at least one expert on personnel administration believes, our real strength as personnel specialists comes from the power of *ideas*.

This chapter will enumerate and briefly describe a set of ideas on what top management or the director of personnel could do to change the direction, tone, staffing, and modus operandi of personnel administration. The list concludes with some suggested milestones to watch for in measuring progress toward the ultimate objective of making personnel administration a more effective integral part of total management.

1. Generate a Commitment

The first step is a bold, non-hedging commitment to reform personnel administration. Without this, all subsequent steps are a wasteful use of resources. The commitment must be made by top management, in writing, and publicized for the information of all concerned. It should pledge a full-scale review of all personnel functions, services, policies and practices, organization, facilities, and staff qualifications in relation to new position descriptions and qualification standards.

2. Conduct a Self-Appraisal Exercise

There should next come a thorough self-appraisal of the way in which personnel administration has been functioning. Personnel specialists themselves deserve a chance to be heard and to put things in order in their own house before the reform effort is extended.

I recently was asked to look at the personnel operations of a local government serving 500,000 residents. My first step was to ask the personnel staff to look at itself and to make recommendations for any changes it deemed appropriate. I offered the following checklist of 32 areas of concern:

Organization and functions of the personnel department.
Selection of director of personnel and senior staff.

Staffing complement and funding level.
How does the personnel office create a presence (role) in day-to-day operations of the county departments and agencies? Examples of its responsiveness?
Are policies and procedures clearly documented in a codified issuance system?
To what extent, if at all, does the personnel department advise top management on organizational patterns?
Classification of positions.
Setting pay levels.
Benefits.
Manpower planning.
Recruitment.
Selection.
Transfers and promotions.
Training, education, and career development.
Incentives (e.g., annual productivity improvement factor as basis for bonuses).
Rewarding high producers.
Dealing with low producers.
Labor–management relations.
Equal employment opportunity.
CETA.
Employee relations.
Firing of employees for cause.
Turnover experience.
Outplacement services.
Records and reports.
Communications (house organs, special issuances, etc.).
Health, safety, and welfare.
Work hours and leave.
Performance appraisal.
Space and work environment.
Evidence of professional qualifications of personnel staff and its continuing growth.

Evidence of methods improvement in personnel.

To what extent is the personnel department actively promoting the flow of beneficial suggestions from employees through Work Simplification and other systematic means?

3. Administer an Internal Survey of User Satisfaction

No principle in American democracy is sounder than that of involving the people affected in the formulation of better ways to have themselves served. This principle, which goes by various names such as "citizen participation" and "participative management," can be put to work in reforming personnel administration. After the personnel specialists have had an opportunity to do some introspective reflection on how well they are serving their clients, it is vital that these users of personnel services be involved in the reform effort.

There is, of course, no standardized method for getting user input. The one I commend most highly requires the use of survey techniques used by professional research groups that gather facts and opinions for the analysis and use of decision makers. A survey questionnaire with a pretested set of precisely worded questions is used by trained interviewers to gather the data from a carefully selected sample of respondents who are representative of the larger population. The encounter between interviewer and each respondent occurs in a private place, and the identity of the respondent is kept absolutely confidential. The number of respondents should be statistically significant, and the sample should be stratified to reach respondents at diverse levels of supervision and management in both line operations and staff services groups.

Essentially, the internal survey seeks to find the gap, if any, between expectations of users of the personnel department and its branches on the one hand and actual personnel services on the other. For example, one respondent may say he expects help from the personnel office in recruitment but seldom receives it; another may say she needs help in handling grievances and does in fact get excellent help.

Respondents can be asked to grade their satisfaction with personnel services on a percentage scale. The difference between what the users expect of personnel administration and what they feel they are actually getting is the *gap* that the reform effort should, of course, seek to close. Obviously, allowances should be made for expressed needs that are completely out of line with a reasonable concept of personnel administration.

The internal survey should not stop with a sample of line and staff officials, but should extend to two other major groups that look to the personnel office for help. One is the entire labor force itself, regardless of title or level of responsibility. Every employee depends on the personnel office for certain services. Soundings should be taken among the employees at large to determine the gap, if any, that exists between their expectations and the services they actually get. The other major group is job applicants. A sample of job applicants should be approached to find out what impressions they gained from their encounters with the personnel office.

4. Purge Inappropriate Functions and Add Others

Chapter 4 discussed the functions of personnel administration I consider "mainline." It also mentioned several that I believe should be dropped due to a long history of neglect, and a few others that we should annex from a homesteader's claim standpoint. Until the personnel department is "purified," we will continue to dissipate some of our energies in border disputes. This realignment of functions has to be negotiated with the organizational-control arm of top management, and the results of the negotiation must be disseminated through the official issuance system.

5. Design a New Organization

The personnel department should be a model organization from an organizational theory standpoint. My own best thinking on the ideal organization and set of functions is set forth in Chapter 4. This organization should be adapted, not adopted, by any organization committed to reform.

There are some principles one will note in studying my array of functions and the organizational format. I prefer flat to tall organizations (no deputies, for example), a clean separation between the thinkers and the doers, a reasonable span of control, and independent check and balance. Organizational elements should be elastic enough to support a few additional people and related functions; they should be rigid enough to provide accountability for results. They should be so constituted as to provide a diamond-shaped career cone of growth opportunities for junior professionals entering at the lower levels; that is, such individuals should not have to leave the specialized field prematurely in order to advance to new levels of responsibility for which they have demonstrated a readiness.

6. Review and Revise Position Descriptions

A well-conceived and written position description is the best known way of defining the duties and responsibilities of a particular "desk" in an organizational setting. So much can flow from that single document once it is written, reviewed, and officially approved. The drafting should be done after full consultation with the present incumbent, if any, with present and prospective supervisors of the work to be done, and with a top management representative who has the broadest perspective.

A controversy has raged for years as to whether position descriptions should be long or short. I favor longer ones over abbreviated ones. The description should begin with a concise general statement of the purpose of the position, and this should be followed by a rather detailed enumeration of *illustrative* duties and responsibilities. Each of these should begin with an action verb that clearly suggests how the work is to be advanced. Loose and vague terms such as "assists" should be avoided. Provision should be made at the end for special assignments.

A brief concluding statement should define the latitude for independent judgment, the amount of supervision over others, outside contacts, and the basic qualifications needed. The position description is a statement of the what, where, when, and who of the body of work to be done; it is not a how-to statement.

7. Review and Revise Qualification Standards

Standards against which to select individuals to fill particular positions are indispensable. It is better to waive or modify standards knowingly than to have no standards at all. Standards, too, should not be developed in a vacuum but with the advice and consent of supervision and management echelons that may have a valid interest in the ultimate performance of persons who may in the future occupy the positions. For example, it can make a great deal of difference whether the standard calls for someone who has been professionally educated as a vocational counselor and has a specified number of years of progressively responsible experience in the field or whether it merely calls for several years of personnel clerk experience.

Qualification standards should be concrete and specific in terms of educational background, relevant work experience, equivalencies, substitutables, special skills such as foreign languages, equipment proficiency, licenses, and any personal features such as age group and sex, to the extent that a valid case can be made for differentiation. There may also be a place in the standard for a statement of the conditions under which the work is to be performed, for instance, stress, noise, dust, or frequent travel.

8. Develop a Policies-and-Procedures Manual

The best of personnel policies and procedures can lead to chaos unless they are systematically laid down in a manual and distributed in readable language to the users. The manual must be well organized, indexed, loose-leaf, and printed in large type on pages with plenty of white space on the borders. Completed forms (simulated) should be included. Flowcharts should be used in the manual to show processing steps and the disposition of copies of action documents. Every page should be dated, and a system for showing readily distinguishable text changes should be installed and explained in the foreword.

The manual should be be read by the users in draft form, and they should be given an opportunity to offer refinements before it is approved for printing. Ideally, a training session should be scheduled to introduce the manual to inexperienced users or when massive changes are introduced to regular users.

9. Select the Director of Personnel and Review His or Her Nominations for Senior Staff Positions

Chapter 4 set forth some key conditions for this staffing operation, including the primary source from which to recruit candidates and six basic competencies against which to measure them. I am convinced that in-house talent, carefully selected against the qualification standards suggested in Chapter 4, will produce better leadership for the personnel program and better end results in the eyes of top management than a group of "imports" whose bio-data may glitter against traditional standards but whose performance may resemble a brief luminous comet.

Selection cannot be hurried. A search committee is a good

idea, because it diffuses responsibility rather than leaving it in the hands of one person. Candidates should be thoroughly briefed by someone who fully understands the new concept of how the personnel department is to function. In particular, they should be made familiar with the idea of serving a fixed tour of duty rather than an indefinite term of service "during good behavior."

The candidates should be afforded an opportunity to tour the central personnel department and one or more of its branches; to talk with subordinate-level employees; to examine personnel files, records, and reports; and to meet with a representative of top management. They should, of course, have access to the self-appraisal survey data and the internal survey data called for earlier in this chapter. Category ratings should be prepared from the full slate of candidates considered.

10. Create a Personnel Department Presence

Chapter 4 discusses a whole series of ways in which an active personnel department can create a presence out in the production arena. Once the new leadership is in place and a philosophy and a set of policies and procedures have been formulated in collaboration with users, it is up to us as personnel specialists to associate ourselves more directly with the producers of goods and services. This cannot be done at some remote, formal place.

There is no standard solution to the need for a presence. I see such possibilities as teams in residence, mobile teams, desks in traffic streams (similar to recruiting desks of the military services in shopping centers), more use of task groups, and more imaginative communication facilities. The idea is to simplify and deformalize the process by which those who need service and support from the personnel department and its branches can get it. A fundamental principle of management is span of control (distance). This says that any management entity will serve and control best those recipient groups which have the closest physical proximity, and that it will tend to neglect those that are more remote.

11. Build an Informed and Responsive Team through Continuing Education

The philosophy and total effectiveness of the senior personnel team depends on a systematic program of training, education, and development. The methods by which a team can be kept current and highly motivated are limited only by the imagination of the team itself and of a coordinator who has the specific responsibility of attending to this matter.

These methods include, but are not limited to, seminars, institutes, workshops, retreats, outside courses, field trips, audiovisual presentations, practical observations, research assignments, speaking engagements, fellowships, sabbaticals, teaching assignments, consultations with visiting experts, and individualized learning through programmed instruction materials and devices.

Job rotation is a method used by some organizations to broaden knowledge and experience. The top personnel positions are ones through which the senior personnel officials can, in my judgment, be rotated. Perhaps two or more tours of duty in the personnel department should be punctuated by a tour back in production operations. It seems to me that a progressive organization can well afford to commit itself in advance to having its senior personnel officials devote a fixed percentage of their careers in training, education, and developmental assignments. A variety of factors would, of course, weigh in the percentage determination.

12. Promote the Adoption and Institutionalization of a Profit-Sharing Plan

Labor Day in the United States calendar has deep significance. To me, it means that the laboring class of people (that's most of us) expects to be reckoned with in the production of goods and services. One of the best ways yet developed for reckoning is through profit-sharing plans that enable the worker to take home a slice of the net profits over and above his base pay and other benefits.

In this connection I am especially impressed with the Scanlon Plan, discussed in Chapter 5. Another individual who has done noteworthy work in this respect is Alan Moganson, who has spearheaded Work Simplification and incentive systems in over 500 companies in the United States, including the highly successful Texas Instruments company. This company reportedly credits at least 10 percent of its annual net profits to the collective gains from Work Simplification suggestions from its employees.

Profit sharing from increased productivity makes such good sense that I am constantly puzzled by the fact that so few companies have adopted this policy. I am therefore planting the yeast for its spread in every personnel department that this book may reach. I hope public agencies will also be moved to do more with incentives. They have done very little, it seems to me, and this may account for some of the citizen dissatisfaction with public services.

13. Install an Efficient Grievance Mechanism

Under the American system of life, the people want their perceived grievances redressed, and they want them redressed with reasonable speed and objectivity. The courts are constantly in trouble because of their backlog of cases pending. But to their credit, they have shown some imagination in trying to cut the waiting time for justice. Examples include small claims courts, the forfeiture of collateral option, creation of special courts to handle cases requiring specialized knowledge (for example, juvenile, domestic relations, and traffic courts). They also use commissioners to prehear cases to save the judges' time.

Employers generally have not been as imaginative in hearing the grievances that accrue to many of the same people during their eight-hour day. Workers can get an expeditious disposition of the accident that happens to them on the way to work, or they can get a hearing on the divorce that may have grown out of the all-night argument the night before the early-morning accident. On the other hand, they may have to wait months or even years to resolve a conflict at the work scene—and the latter may be the root cause of the domestic difficulties, which, in turn, led to the automobile accident and the divorce. This seems, indirectly at least, to be an obstruction of people's constitutionally guaranteed right to the pursuit of happiness.

One approach would be to establish an ombudsman office as an arm of the personnel director's, if not the CEO's, office (preferably the latter). The checks-and-balances principle requires an independent review. Another approach would be the use of a mobile team of hearing examiners who would "ride a circuit." This team could be assembled from a panel of persons approved by both labor and management. More than one team could be operative when the case load demands it. The panel could include a few citizens and one team member could be a citizen.

Obviously, the need to provide swift and objective resolution of grievances must be balanced against the possibility of the system becoming so efficient that it would attract some frivolous cases. Experience is the best basis for dealing with that possibility. To do nothing toward reform on the claim that efficiency begets an unnecessary case load is the ostrich approach to leadership.

14. Set Aside Something for Research and Development

Early American history reveals that during the hard winters, some of the pioneers were inclined to eat their seed corn, thus leaving them dependent on others for the spring planting. I am almost convinced that most of us personnel specialists behave similarly with respect to our obligation to improve the art of personnel administration. It is also apparent to me that we will never be well enough off budgetwise to afford a separate account for research and development. We have to find ways and means of improving the efficiency of operations so as to have something left over to encourage further savings and improvements.

There are other possible sources of money and staff with which to do research and development. One is to sell our clients on allocating a portion of their resources for the cause. After all, they are the ultimate beneficiaries of any breakthroughs brought about by research and development. Another might be organizations with grant money. Finally, there may be graduate students and professors who need a research project with which to test a working hypothesis.

Once a source of funding is discovered, the personnel department can devise working models and orchestrate their trial use through the work of branch offices. Having a first team of personnel administrators who have come from production centers should greatly facilitate the selection of, and concurrence in, test sites.

The whole spectrum of personnel problems lends itself to research and development. For example, the issue of how first-level supervisors should be trained has never been settled to my satisfaction. Why don't we try some new approaches and see what happens in terms of productivity, morale, turnover, accidents, and costs? Personnel administration is indeed a fertile field for some fresh and intelligently conceived research and development.

15. Explore Different Methods of Communication

Stilted, bureaucratic communication can be counterproductive. An imaginative, aggressive personnel team should try different forms of communication until it finds the most effective media. It is not necessarily the written word or the conventional format of meetings and conferences. Why not a forum in which troublesome issues are debated? I believe I learned more from being a member of my high school debating team than I did from any specific course. It is a fascinating means of exploring the pros and cons of an issue.

Another technique that excites thinking is role-playing in front of a videotape camera and a live audience. This has the added advantage of producing an end product that can be disseminated to outreach audiences. Such audiences can, in turn, document their own views on videotape and thus facilitate two-way communication.

Still another way to communicate is to show how a personnel process is expected to work by setting up a demonstration project. For example, the group oral examination has been around for at least 30 years, but some organizations have never tried it. The personnel department could help one of its clients set this method in motion, monitor it, bring other clients to the scene to observe it, and report the results of the demonstration project after it has run for a reasonable period.

I have found annual and special reports to be especially effective as communication tools. One can spotlight the good work done by line and staff groups to improve personnel administration practices and identify some uncharted frontiers. It seems to be an informal means of setting performance standards and encouraging friendly rivalry among the several organizational elements.

The incentive awards program can sometimes by used to identify individuals and groups who have demonstrated extraordinary human capabilities. Appropriate publicity of such awards not only gives recognition to the award recipients but is a means of communicating on such factors as performance standards, selection and training, work methods, and supervision.

16. Put Some Milestones in Place and Record Progress

The design of the evaluation yardsticks needs to be an integral part of the initial conceptual planning process; otherwise it never gets done, or the results are open to question. In this connection, I recently participated in the selection of a chief executive officer of a large organization. One of his first acts after installation was to formulate a comprehensive list of specific performance goals for his first year. He then discussed them widely among his senior staff in order to test the reality of each goal and objective and to convert them into performance goals and objectives of the staff itself. It was an exciting exercise and one that was calculated to turn the organization around in its service program.

Here are some examples of this CEO's management-by-objectives list:

Decrease member turnover rate to 10 percent.

Initiate planning to improve services to adolescents, elderly, and the chronically ill.

Develop a systematic hospital pre-admission testing and discharge planning program.

Develop a program to assess member health care needs and a three-year plan to meet these needs.

Implement a series of in-service education programs for the full board of trustees.

Keep hospital utilization below 420 days per 1,000 members.

Develop a policies-and-procedures manual and ensure its effective use.

Institute a publications policy.

Implement a plan for regular, systematic information flow to the public.

Part III

User Perspectives

Chapter 8

How to Deal with the Personnel Office

IT DISTURBS ME at times to note that a new piece of equipment is accompanied by an operator's manual, whereas the new employee is not. The manual explains the procedure for getting the equipment going and how to obtain the best results. It also has tips on what to do in case of malfunctioning before calling a mechanic. Such is not the case with new employees. Employees arrive and must be accepted on an "as is" basis, even though people are infinitely more complicated than machines.

A leading business journal reported recently that the private sector is reaching for more people-wise executives. It also reports that there is a trend to make the personnel director a member of top management. This book applauds these moves. I am convinced our economy would be farther along the pike if such a value system had evolved sooner. Just as enterprises need experts on production and marketing, they also need experts on people.

This chapter, unfortunately, is not the ultimate manual on how to get the best results from people. It is a "user's manual" with tips, but it is one step removed; it endeavors to teach users of personnel offices—offices with staffs of presumed "people mechanics"—how to use such offices successfully, The "users" are identified as four groups: top management, managers and supervisors, employees generally, and job applicants. Tips are offered from my 40 years of experience in personnel work to each of these groups.

Obviously, there are no sure-fire formulas for making every encounter with the personnel office a happy and productive experience. I promise that users who follow my guidelines will have a better "batting average" in the long run than those who plod along and constantly have a headache from banging their heads against personnel doors.

GUIDELINES FOR TOP MANAGEMENT USERS OF PERSONNEL OFFICES

These guidelines are in the form of general principles rather than specific techniques, for executive styles vary widely. In the discussion that follows, "it" refers, of course, to the central personnel department and its several branches, if any; that is, to the personnel system.

Cut it in on policy and program goals. Policies and programs can change without regard to the calendar or established budget cycle. When possible, the personnel department should be alerted to such changes well in advance of their effective date and, if possible, made a party to the change process. The changes may require the personnel department to act in the job applicant market, adjust compensation, renegotiate labor–management contracts, reduce the labor force, upgrade skills, and the like.

Insist on completed staff work. Some of us in the personnel business do sloppy staff work. We write cryptic and illegible notes. We omit supporting data. We fail to point up the options, pros and cons of each, price tags, and implications. In brief, we have ceased to observe the fundamental rule of completed staff work in our relationship with decision makers. Completed staff work takes more time on our part, but it usually saves more precious time at higher levels and is likely to earn us a better reputation, more face-to-face access to busy executives, and faster disposition of our paperwork.

Make it an active participant. The cliché, "People are down on what they are not up on," applies to personnel officials as much as it does to anyone else. Passive resistance or unenlightened action may be the end result of leaving the personnel department in the dark. If it is felt that the personnel department cannot be trusted with background information, it may be time to make some changes in the lineup in personnel. I can think of no other valid reason for withholding information or not enlisting the active participation of the personnel department in top management moves that affect human resources.

Don't abuse it. Even though the personnel department is in a sense the "servant" of top management, servants deserve respect and the preservation of self-esteem. When we in personnel are asked to develop a "case" for removing an employee from a certain position or from the payroll and no case exists, that is abuse, and sometimes arrogant abuse. When we in personnel are asked to "find a way" to promote a favored employee over others doing identical work of equal or better quality, that is abuse. When we in personnel are asked to summarily change the duty station of an employee in order to "force him to quit," that is abuse. Top management's prerogative to hire and fire is non-negotiable, but when top management decides to exercise this right with reckless abandon, it should shoulder the responsibility for such actions by signing the action documents rather than foisting the task off on the personnel unit.

Require program planning as a way of reducing the case-oriented outlook. The misery of a growing case load in a personnel office begets more misery. Each new case seems to loom larger than the last. It is like the reorder and customer complaint volume in a sluggish materials procurement pipeline. I am convinced that a good remedy for all of this is systematic program planning. Top management should see to it that we don't slip out of the program planning habit and into the case-handling habit.

Demand good reporting and accountability. We in personnel have no difficulty grinding out statistical data on our operations, but we are not so mindful of our responsibility for substantive, analytical reports. One good summary conclusion sentence or paragraph, supported by analyzed data, can equal a pound of raw, meaningless statistics. Comparative material by organizational element for a given reporting period may be more valuable than the composite picture, or at least it could be furnished as a supplement. At the end of a logical accounting period, we should rack up our accomplishments in parallel with our preset goals for the same period, and we should explain objectively why we slipped on some and exceeded expectations on others. Such reports should end with solid recommendations to top management for both the short-term and long-range periods ahead in each major phase of personnel administration.

Continue the development of its staff. Perhaps the single best solution to the problems that beset many of us in personnel work is an intelligent staff development plan. This involves, I believe, a jointly developed and approved individual development plan for each member of the professional staff, and continual inputs of employer-sponsored in-service training matched by appropriate self-education, self-training, and self-improvement. The plan, like that for any other group of employees, should aim to broaden and deepen knowledge, skills, and attitudes.

GUIDELINES FOR LINE OFFICIALS AND OTHER STAFF OFFICIALS AS USERS OF PERSONNEL OFFICES

Much of what has just been said for the benefit of top management applies equally to this second audience. My general advice would go something like this: coordinate in the early stages, level with it, become involved, don't abuse it, and use it rather than short-circuit it. Specific suggestions follow.

Borrow staff. We in the personnel office frequently lack the perspective we need to act intelligently as partners to our operating friends. There is no substitute for an in-residence work experience to fill this gap. Just as a series of foreign assignments builds foreign service officers of the U.S. State Department, and a series of rotating field and staff assignments of military officers builds military leadership, on-site special assignments away from the personnel office can build personnel administrators. Textbooks, courses, and conferences offer a bare minimum of the insights needed. Therefore, I believe personnel administration is strengthened and operations personnel gain when a line or staff official can negotiate the detail of a personnel specialist for a specific project of work. The host office should extend the invitation—in writing.

Go joint-venture. The personnel department will never be staffed and funded sufficiently to accomplish independently all that needs doing about human resources. It has to be a joint venture. Besides, control of the purse strings gives the operating people all the control needed to shape the action plan to their goals and objectives. The personnel department should have a seasoned corps of personnel generalists and specialists from which a member can be spun off to join an on-site operations team. The "battle ribbon" with which the personnel representative returns to his own camp will enhance his peers as well; additionally, it will provide him with a sense of fulfillment.

Assign tasks and set targets. Production people are thoroughly accustomed to contracting with outside sources for goods and services. I suggest they use this principle in dealing internally with staff groups such as the personnel department. The contract format has a "scope of work" element as the heart of the understanding as to what is to be done. It may provide for a series of sequential task orders, each with its own peculiar requirements, limitations, and target deadlines. I believe this approach can be transferred to personnel business and is worth a try where communication with, and performance by, personnel staffs has been a problem. Obviously this is not needed for every personnel action, but a formal agreement may be useful in connection with a program goal or objective with a distinct beginning and end.

Ask for internal audits. I recently reviewed a personnel system where the operating officials had to wait up to seven years for organization and classification audits. Don't accept that kind of situation. Changes in program emphasis, adjustments in organization, and advances in technology all can cause massive obsolescence in position descriptions and compensation relationships. It takes broadside, systematic desk audits to spot the incongruities. The tendency of the personnel office, due to exessive workload and rigidity of budgets, is to let such audits go year after year and merely audit isolated individual positions on which there is pressure to review. This produces inequities in compensation, affects turnover and recruitment adversely, and disturbs morale and productivity.

Enlist outside help. One of the most popular ways to reduce the possibility of mistakes in surgery and to reduce health costs is the practice of getting a second opinion from a medical specialist without a vested interest in the case. Line and staff officials might well put this principle to work with respect to major personnel administration decisions.

For example, I once assembled a panel of industrial training experts to review the prospects for training 140,000 enumerators at 5,000 locations in the United States prior to the beginning of a decennial census. The results were reassuring both for the operating officials, who were furnishing the funds and who were most interested in the quality of the statistical products, and for me as the training specialist who had designed the training plan.

Commend it. The personnel office is not as bad as its image suggests in many quarters. Where its performance is at least spotty, something ought to be made of the bright spots. Line and staff officials who from time to time see a brilliant piece of work done by one of us could be supportive by sending a note of acknowledgment. I see a monthly list of compliments and criticisms of the performance of the medical staff of the health care organization of which I am a trustee. The 110,000 members fire off many more criticisms than they do compliments, but you would be surprised how far a single well-earned compliment travels. The medical director sends a copy to the interested physician or technician, with a copy to the employee's official personnel folder and an information copy to the trustees and other key staff members. It has a refreshing effect.

Lend it some expertise. The practice of lending resource people for joint-venture projects can be a two-way street. Instead of inviting the personnel department to place a specialist in residence in your area of operations, it may be more appropriate to detail an operations expert to the personnel office.

For example, the personnel people may be running a recruitment scheme in which an operations person would be a logical teammate to an employment specialist. Or it may be developing an audiovisual program or a brochure in which the practical experience of an operator is needed. Procedural changes may require consultation with operations experts. Such loans cultivate continuing good relationships and add a measure of quality assurance to things done in the personnel office.

Invite representation. A necessary part of any operating official's cost of doing business, I believe, is that of keeping the supporting staff groups informed on current operations and future plans. One of the easiest ways to do this is to invite representation at significant events from the personnel office and other appropriate staff groups.

For example, if a major operating department is staging a quarterly conference of its regional officials, why not budget some time on the agenda for a personnel representative on a timely topic? It need not be a solo performance with a prepared speech. The assignment can be as a panelist, a buzz session resource person, or a question-and-answer commentator in plenary sessions. Everybody can gain something from this exchange, and the gesture of inviting personnel representation will be greatly appreciated.

Build good records. Discipline in any organization depends upon the ability of the individual in charge to fire people who need to be fired. If a department head has the right to hire and fire, it follows that he or she has the right to keep records that track each employee's performance on the job and any behavioral patterns and incidents that reflect favorably or unfavorably upon the organization and the employee. Such records form the best basis for commendations and promotions on the one hand and for penalty actions on the other.

It is a sad state of affairs at the operating level when managers have empty files, or no files, to support their plea to the personnel office to "do something about ______!" Some personnel offices, including those of the U.S. government, discourage supervisors and managers from keeping duplicate personnel folders pertaining to conduct and work performance of employees. These personnel offices seem to want an absolute monopoly on information about the employee, leaving those who have the primary concern for employee preformance empty-handed. This is absurd and may well account for many of the cases of "untouchables" who should have been fired years ago.

Institute a practical performance appraisal system. This is another phase of personnel administration on which we have not been very helpful to operating officials. In talking with officials in two large departments in a political jurisdiction of a half million inhabitants recently, I learned that they regard the performance appraisal system imposed by the personnel department as a joke. We tend to become enamored of a *form* or a *formula* for totaling one's performance over a reporting period, usually a year. We use a *sign language*, such as plus, minus, and check mark. We use descriptive *adjectives* and *phrases*. We usually end up tossing 98 percent or more of the employees into a broad and meaningless category, such as "satisfactory."

Again, I recommend a system analogous to the concept of a contract. The supervisor needs a clear understanding with each employee on the expectations of the organization from anyone who performs the duties and responsibilities of that position. This will need to be expressed differently for each class and level of work. In a clerical position, where output can be quantified, it may be stated as the number of work units to be processed per hour or per day, and the error allowance (say, 2 percent). In a professional position, where measurement of results has to be more subjective, the understanding or "contract" may have to be expressed in terms of objectives, projects to be started and finished, resource limitations not to be exceeded, target dates for completion of steps and entire projects, and the like. This understanding needs to be recorded in writing, even if merely by informal notes initialed by both parties.

Three more features of a practical system deserve a note. Performance appraisal should, of course, serve a valid purpose and not be just a meaningless exercise. It is directly related to the issue of the appraised employee's potential, his training needs (both immediate and long-term), and his promotability. Therefore, it should address these questions in plain English, not sign language.

Level with it. There are only a few individuals in our society with whom we are accustomed to leveling. The number is short by at least one—the personnel representative. Ministers, physicians, and attorneys are perhaps the three disciplines with which people tend to level the most. Spiritual well-being, health, and freedom from legal difficulties are guarded closely.

Every operating official should be willing to take the personnel representative completely into his confidence and let the results rest on the merits of the case for the action proposed; otherwise, we in personnel are as handicapped as the favored practitioners would be with only part of the facts at hand. If it were a case of all hands not being clean, you would be surprised at how much company you would have at a confessional. Your leveling would be such a refreshing experience for both the personnel representative and yourself that when the issue is resolved, win or lose, you will delight in having committed yourself to forthright dealings where the career future of human beings is at stake.

Don't abuse it. The comment already made for top management (see the preceeding section) applies equally to line and staff officials.

Keep it informed. When you make the commitment to go joint-venture with another organizational element and to level with it on difficult occasions, then it follows that you need to keep it currently informed at all times. I recently traveled some 2,000 miles by chartered bus and ferry through the beautiful countries of Norway, Sweden, and Denmark with 37 other people, including a tour guide with whom all of us were deeply impressed. Two of her great strengths were her ease of communication (no less than six languages) and her thoughtfulness in singling out individuals with special needs and interests. She used a technique of posting, within minutes after arrival in each new city, what she called her "love letter" to our group near the elevator in the lobby of the hotel. It had daily instructions and suggestions for making our stay most productive and comfortable. Operating officials could dramatically improve their relations with the personnel office by writing, calling, sending notes, or posting a summary digest of developments with manpower implications.

Relate to someone. Many of us in personnel strike out because we get a chance to perform only on assignments reflected off the personnel director's desk. Instead of getting the problem straight from the operating official, we often get from the personnel director or his secretary a sketchy version of what happened or what is needed. Instead of trying to find out who is to blame for this state of affairs, I urge operating officials to wean themselves away from the personnel director and search out a personnel specialist with whom to deal on each major type of personnel problem. What a joy it is to find someone with whom to deal regularly in a good specialty store such as a hardware store. It can work just as smoothly in the personnel office.

Support it. The minister, the physician, and the attorney all have a personal need from time to time for support from others in their respective professions, and even from the constituencies they serve. Operating officials should likewise reverse the flow of support to personnel officials when circumstances dictate. The personnel department is subject to the same abuse as protective agencies of government. A steady barrage of abuse can have a debilitating effect on personnel people's morale and will to work. It is less than humanitarian not to share the burden, not to give credit where credit is due, and not to lend a helping hand when the load is heavy.

Support begets support. It is only human for the personnel people to support first and foremost those who reciprocate. Why not feed it a few success stories about employees to whose success on the job it contributed in some way, so that the message can go out to other audiences?

Feed its communication media. The personnel office tires of publishing house organs with bland news or no news. It obviously can't support a big staff of paid reporters; it must rely on operating officials to alert it to newsworthy events and to help with the reporting tasks. House organs can be of tremendous value in building morale internally and goodwill externally. After all, whole families have access to such publications, and they talk and travel. It is an inexpensive means of having your own operations spotlighted.

GUIDELINES FOR EMPLOYEES ON HOW TO MAKE BETTER USE OF THEIR PERSONNEL OFFICE

My advice in general terms to employee users of personnel offices is to get acquainted with the personnel staff, keep informed of personnel affairs through their diverse media, and by all means use their services. More specifically, I suggest the following.

Establish a focal point. You cannot possibly deal with all members of the personnel staff about all matters affecting your own interests. You have to establish yourself with someone in particular and focus your inquiries. Use that person as a referral agent until you learn who does what. The relationship is almost identical to the way in which you work with the medical world to maintain your health. Your personal physician knows you better than anyone else, and from time to time he or she will refer you to a specialist. Your point of contact in personnel is logically with a member of the employee relations staff, but there is no rule against your dealing with a member of another group.

Study the relevant laws. There are many federal, state, and local laws that affect one's rights and responsibilities as a worker in the business world. Given that we are a nation ruled by laws, I suppose some case could be made for requiring everyone to be versed in constitutional provisions and the laws of the land. This, of course, is not very practical; but any intelligent person who has reasonable reading comprehension abilities can search out and familiarize himself with the laws that affect his current employment and future Social Security and retirement benefits.

Look at this example of how such knowledge can pay off. I recently was invited to counsel an individual who felt she was due some back pay for having been detailed to work at a higher level of responsibility. The employer brushed aside her formal request for back pay with the answer that she wasn't eligible for it. I researched the applicable laws and regulations and found that there was indeed a solid basis for her claim. I drafted her appeal, and after several months she received a written response affirming her eligibility for an amount which I estimate could run close to $10,000. Better still, the series of details occurred near the end of the appellant's active service just before retirement. Through the appeal, she also earned the right to have her lifetime retirement annuity recomputed, using the higher temporary salary as a part of her multiplier in the retirement formula. Thus, this woman will receive a higher pension for the rest of her life. The moral to this true story is that it pays to know the law—or someone who does.

Learn the ground rules. Any organization of considerable size is likely to have a personnel policies-and-procedures manual. Other issuances include the position classification standards, position qualification standards, and labor–management agreements. These documents are the ground rules by which all personnel actions are effected. They change rather frequently; in fact, far more often than the laws they interpret. Therefore, you have to read these reference aids carefully. Find out where the nearest copy is kept and reexamine it several times each year to see what changes have occurred (oftener if you hear of significant changes having been made). In case your nearest manual owner objects to your browsing through his copy, you can always find a copy in the organization's library or personnel office.

A good personnel manual has a clever system for signaling recent changes in language, and every page is dated. It also has a detailed table of contents and an index. Should you ever consider taking your claim for redress on a personnel matter to court, the judge will first want to know whether or not you have exhausted your administrative remedies. The personnel manual tells you what they are.

Follow the in-house media. The personnel office generally uses, as continuing information sources, such media as in-house newspapers or magazines, bulletin boards, special notices, audiovisual presentations, pay envelope slips, employee handbooks, and reports. You can glean useful information from all these sources, and it is well to build a file of them for future reference. One gains a certain amount of authority and peer respect by having quick access to reliable information sources.

Feed your file. Your official personnel file in the personnel office mirrors your knowledge, skills, abilities, work experience, performance, training, education and development experiences, personal history, and the recognition you have received for outstanding accomplishments. Unfortunately, some of the ablest employees in the business world have only skeleton personnel files. The employee himself, when he neglects to report significant developments, is partially to blame, and that neglect can affect his future career opportunities.

It is better to over-report than to under-report. Examples of things that might not seem worth reporting are: inventions, authorship, licenses, hobbies, foreign travel, foreign languages acquired, civic awards, promotion in military reserves, and community leadership roles. You may want to ask that a special field assignment report of which you are particularly proud be added to your file.

Propose solutions in writing. From time to time, you may want to write and present constructive thoughts to your personnel office on some matter on which the personnel regulations are silent or ambiguous. A good format includes three paragraph headings: the problem, discussion, and recommendation. A few of these memoranda to your personnel office, and it will realize that there is at least one sharp observer among its clientele. You may get a call to come by and discuss the matter in greater depth with either the personnel officer or a member of the personnel staff. If a reply is made to your communication in writing, a copy will doubtless go to your personnel file, and this can later be a credit.

Enlist in personnel endeavors. A subtle way to further your objective of becoming known in a favorable light in the personnel office is to find opportunities to volunteer for extracurricular duty on projects under personnel auspices. You will need to clear all such arrangements with your supervisor.

On one occasion you may be a recruitment team member or a selection panelist. On another, you may appear as a Speaker's Bureau representative to help build goodwill in the community by interpreting the mission of your enterprise. If you are recreation-oriented, you may want to volunteer to organize an intramural athletic team such as bowling or tennis. If you have a flair for writing or photography, you may want to develop a feature story for a house organ on some facet of the organization's work.

Avail yourself of the services. A well-conceived and well-managed personnel office offers a wide variety of services and benefits to employees of the organization it serves. If these services go begging, they are soon curtailed or dropped. For example, one of the greatest needs of many young adults in the business world, and even of mature adults at selected junctures of life, is that of career counseling. If a personnel office has never had a request for career counseling, or if it hires a career counselor outright but never generates any business for the individual, this great need continues unfulfilled.

If a health unit in the personnel office establishes a clinic or a capability for physical examinations and employees pass it by, this is unfortunate. If the personnel office invites in a series of experts on problems that retiring employees are likely to encounter and the meetings have to be canceled for lack of interest, the personnel people—and you, if you are within a few years of retirement—are the losers. If the personnel office has an expert in residence on selected occasions to explain vital issues such as taxes, health and insurance provisions, and new union agreement terms and you boycott the session, another opportunity has been lost. The same can be said for employee training and development offerings and many other services.

GUIDELINES FOR JOB APPLICANTS IN USING PERSONNEL OFFICES

Many job applicants are naively unaware of the fact that all hiring is not done by the personnel office. They believe that the proper thing to do is to take one's credentials to the receptionist in the personnel office, wait one's turn to see an interviewer, respond as well as possible to the interviewer's questions, take a performance test if one is required, leave, and await a yes or no answer by letter or telephone. This is one pattern, but it is frequently appropriate only for the lowest-level positions such as stenographer, clerk-typist, or manual laborer.

Here are some practical tips for job applicants who are inclined to start their job search with the personnel office.

Establish a beachhead in operations. Don't stop at the personnel office. The real power and resources in any organization reside where the substantive work is done—not in the staff support offices such as personnel. This means out in the departments, divisions, and branches where such basic processes as research, design, production, inspection, marketing, and transportation are in progress. Use your best imagination to think of a way to meet some of these officials and to show them what you can do best.

Impossible, you may think. Not so. I know a young woman who used her professor to help her establish a beachhead in a large organization, where her initial assignment was a summer internship. During that summer, she met, impressed, and performed well for some important people of the organization. Step by step, she climbed and gained more security and status. After less than five years, she had permanent status, at slightly under $30,000 annual salary plus attractive fringe benefits. All of this happened, in my judgment, because this young woman was well qualified, established a beachhead at the right place at the right time, and concentrated on proving herself.

I have just negotiated with a sociology professor to deploy six or seven of his students in a survey of the effectiveness of a large personnel administration program. As these students conduct private, in-depth interviews with executives and managers, they may well impress someone with hiring authority who will make a mental note to look at one of them later for possible employment. Work-study assignments, summer internships, and research projects are all good avenues for beachhead purposes.

Avoid power plays. It is always tempting to have a political figure, a union leader, a veterans group, or someone else in a strong influential position to intervene on your behalf as a job applicant. The use of such power plays is bad strategy. Even if it gets you the job you are after, it more or less marks you as someone who will continue to apply pressure—for promotions, choice assignments, and special privileges. The employer knows that you will be capable of undermining your supervisor's authority, including any action he or she may take to discipline or dismiss you. Employers avoid unnecessary risks by just not hiring power players. Power plays are counterproductive.

Don't hassle. After you have a commitment from an operating official to have your appointment processed by the personnel office, it is well to let the process follow its due course through the clearance channels. Don't try to rush it by agitating or hassling the individuals in the circuitry. You can imagine the chaos if everyone with an action in the mill were to begin pushing and shoving his case along. Personnel employees have a long memory, for they have a habit of making notes in a file every time someone nudges them on a case.

A better course of action is to be painstaking in the completion of all documents required by the personnel office, let them know how to reach you at all times, and respond immediately to any follow-through inquiries. Let your contact in operations, where you expect to work, decide whether or not and when to apply pressure to expedite your case. Of course, that office should apply any pressure it decides is needed.

Use the interim time well. There may be several days, or even weeks, between the commitment to hire and your actual entrance on duty. Some people take off for the beach or the mountains in order to get some rest before making a fresh start. This may be all right, but there are some things to be done even if they have to be done at the beach or the mountains.

In your visits to the employer's place during the job negotiations, you will probably have collected some material for pre-orientation purposes. Use the waiting period to read and absorb it. Call for more if the first batch whets your appetite for more answers. It will make a good impression in the early stages of your employment if your working vocabulary and knowledge of what goes on clearly reveal that you have done some reading.

A second thing you should do without fail is this. I am convinced that every major employment experience should be a purposeful building block in one's growth and development. Therefore, it behooves you to reflect on your immediate past employment and then on your total past employment. If there has been no past employment experience, then reflect on your total educational experience. What can you look back on with the most pride of accomplishment? Why? What are your real strengths? Weaknesses? What specific objectives do you have for the new job? How long do you think you'll need to accomplish what you want to accomplish in the new job? How will it fit into your personal plan for systematic growth and development? How can you overcome your known weaknesses and further add to your known strengths?

These reflections, if honestly made between innings in your work history, may enable you to gain time and accelerate your move up the career ladder. I am confident they will.

Index